ar 2-16-76

Milton and the English Mind

"As good almost kill a man as kill a good book:
who kills a man kills a reasonable creature, God's
image; but he who destroys a good book, kills reason itself, kills the image of God, as it were, in the
eye. Many a man lives a burden to the earth; but a
good book is the precious life-blood of a master-
spirit, embalmed and treasured up on purpose to a
life beyond life."

from *Areopagitica*

Men and History

Collier Books ready or in preparation

F. E. Hutchinson, D.Litt., F.B.A.

(Sometime Fellow of All Souls College, Oxford)

MILTON AND THE ENGLISH MIND

COLLIER BOOKS

NEW YORK, N.Y.

This Collier Books edition is published by arrangement with The Macmillan Company

Collier Books is a division of The Crowell-Collier Publishing Company

First Collier Books Edition 1962

This title first appeared as a volume in the Teach Yourself History series under the general editorship of A. L. Rowse

Contents

Contents

To the Reader

As THIS BOOK takes its place in an historical series, I have devoted as much space to Milton's ideas—political, social and religious—as to his poetry. If the chapters on his religious beliefs appear technical, they are not included in the interests of orthodoxy, but because both the poetry and the prose writings of Milton, as of most writers in the seventeenth century on political and social problems, have a theological background which is largely unfamiliar, and perhaps uncongenial, to many readers of the present day.

I have quoted liberally; partly because there is little use in discussing the poems without quoting from them; partly because the most authentic testimony about Milton's life and aims is to be sought in the autobiographical passages scattered through his voluminous treatises. I have throughout given the references to the passages quoted. For the treatises I have referred to the cheap and convenient edition of Bohn, although I have generally taken my English quotations from the original editions, and the translations from the Latin are not always those to be found in Bohn.

F. E. H.

Milton and the English Mind

Chapter 1

Johannes Milton, Anglus

JOHN MILTON is not only among the greatest of our poets, but he is also a great and representative Englishman. No writer has expressed his faith in England with greater eloquence and conviction that Milton. As a true patriot, he warned his countrymen if he saw them being unfaithful to their high destiny. He has expressed the English mind in his lifelong advocacy of freedom. It is for freedom—civil, political and religious—that the English people have made their most determined struggles. Milton is also very English in the importance which he always attached to moral issues. He saw religious and political questions as a matter of right and wrong, and never doubted his own rightness. This conviction made him unable to recognize virtue and conscience in his opponents, but his concern for righteousness is in itself a characteristic which Englishmen have commonly admired in their spokesmen.

Milton lived in a time of the greatest political upheaval which England has ever known, and he took his side. This partisanship has made it difficult for those who do not share his opinions to do justice to him as a man or as a poet. Some of them, to their loss, have deprived themselves of the happiness and inspiration of appreciating a very great poet. The wiser of them have made the right allowances for the heat of the times. If they question Milton's application of high principles to particular issues, they have recognized that the principles themselves of political freedom and religious toleration have since won the general acceptance of Englishmen of all parties and creeds.

If Milton was a Puritan, he was also more than a Puritan. He was a humanist who had steeped himself in the literature of Greece and Rome, besides making himself acquainted with the finest products of the Italian Renaissance. There was, indeed, some unresolved tension in his mind between his hu-

11

manism and his Puritanism, between the appeal of Hellenic and of Hebrew influences. His culture was broadly based. He received at St. Paul's School and at Cambridge the best education that the times afforded, and he furthered his studies by foreign travel. He had talked with Grotius and Galileo, and with Manso, the friend and patron of Tasso. Distinguished foreign scholars corresponded with him and sought his personal acquaintance. His friendships at home were confined to no narrow circle. Sir Henry Wotton was one of the first to discern his poetic gifts and to encourage him, and Andrew Marvell was a younger colleague of his in the service of the State. His father has a place among the madrigal-writers who were a glory of the Elizabethan age, and the young Milton was twice associated with Henry Lawes.

No English poet, not even Wordsworth, has provided the biographer and interpreter with more first-hand testimony about himself than Milton. His character and aims can be clearly discerned because he has revealed himself, indirectly in his poems and directly in his prose writings. It is allowable to recognize many of the lineaments of John Milton in his portrayal of Christ and Satan, of Adam and Samson. It may appear strange to us, but not to this man so fully persuaded of his own virtue and consummate ability, to interpolate long autobiographical passages in his treatises. In the exposition of his theory of church government he dilates at length on the dedication of his powers to poetry and on his personal character, and he turns aside in his *Defence of the English People* to defend himself. We see what manner of man he believed himself to be, and the accounts of him given by his two nephews and the known facts of his life go far to corroborate his own estimate. There is something of "plain Heroic magnitude of mind" in his resolute postponement of his poetic ambitions until he had served what he believed to be the more urgent call of the State, and in the resumption of his cherished task after twenty years in spite of blindness, age, impoverished estate and the frustration of his political and religious hopes. Adversity would sober his faith, but could not break his spirit. He might have boldly claimed for himself the divine approbation pronounced upon the seraph Abdiel:

> Servant of God, well done, well hast thou fought
> The better fight, who single hast maintaind
> Against revolted multitudes the Cause
> Of Truth, in word mightier than they in Armes.
>
> (P.L., VI, 29)[1]

The sternness which enabled him to face defeat, obloquy and danger, developed in him the harder strain in his character at the expense of tenderness, and made him an exacting husband and parent, and an unsparing controversialist. He has won men's admiration more than their love.

[1] P.L. is used for excerpts from *Paradise Lost* throughout this book.

Chapter 2

John Milton's Education

THOUGH JOHN MILTON was born and died a Londoner, he came of yeoman stock in the near neighbourhood of Oxford. The family tradition shows in each generation the independence of their religious thinking. The poet's grandfather Richard Milton, of Stanton St. John, adhered to the old faith and was fined as a recusant in 1601. His son John, the poet's father, after some education at Oxford, conformed to the Church of England and was promptly disinherited. With the help of a friend or relatives he established himself as a scrivener in London. The scrivener's was then a profession in which, besides mere copying for laywers and other clients, he prepared leases, deeds and other straightforward documents such as would now fall to a solicitor to do.

John Milton the elder prospered and was able to retire with "a plentiful estate" in the year that his elder son John left Cambridge. He was a man of culture with a special delight in music which he communicated to his son. He has his own little title to remembrance, beyond what he did for his son: to Morley's famous set of madrigals in praise of Queen Elizabeth, *The Triumphs of Oriana,* he contributed a six-part madrigal, "Fayre Oriana in the Morne," and madrigals and motets of his are in other collections. His son's lifelong interest in music is apparent in many happy allusions in his poetry to that art and in the singularly musical quality of his verse. The poet followed up this study in his early manhood, and on his Italian tour shipped home "a chest or two of choice music books," and we learn from Aubrey that he had "a delicate and tuneable voice." Even the austere poet, at least in his earlier years, could be wooed to gentler mood by "the pealing Organ" and "the full voic'd Quire" which

> Dissolve me into extasies,
> And bring all Heav'n before mine eyes.

He even allows the fallen angels some share in the delights of music. We might expect "Sonorous mettal blowing Martial sounds," when Satan's legions gather for battle, but there is nothing heavenly in such brazen music. There is, however, better music to follow:

> Anon they move
> In perfect *Phalanx* to the *Dorian* mood
> Of Flutes and soft Recorders; such as rais'd
> To highth of noblest temper Heros old
> Arming to Battel.
>
> (P.L., I, 549.)

The Dorian was approved by Plato as "the true Hellenic mode," and when Milton is considering in the *Areopagitica* what would be required if music as well as books were to be licensed, he says: "No musick must be heard, no song be set or sung, but what is grave and *Dorick*" (B., II, 73).[2] And when the fallen angels have leisure for recreation, the milder of them betake themselves to music, for they were angels, though fallen, and had not lost all their "Original brightness."

> Others more milde,
> Retreated in a silent valley, sing
> With notes Angelicall to many a Harp
> Thir own Heroic deeds and hapless fall . . .
> Thir song was partial, but the harmony
> (What could it less when Spirits immortal sing?)
> Suspended Hell, and took with ravishment
> The thronging audience.
>
> (P.L., II, 546.)

Milton was singularly fortunate in his parentage, and he has amply and repeatedly acknowledged his debt. There is a fine tribute to his father in his Latin poem *Ad Patrem*; he thinks it not strange that father and son should pursue "cognate arts," for, as he had shown in his early ode, "At a Solemn Musick," music and poetry are "Sphear-born harmonious Sisters" who are bidden: "Wed your divine sounds." In the *Second Defence of the English People* he proudly says: "My father was distinguished by the undeviating integrity of

[2] B. is used for references to Bohn's Standard Edition of *Milton's Prose Works*.

his life; my mother, by the esteem in which she was held, and the alms which she bestowed" (B., I, 254).

In his father's house in Bread Street, Cheapside, with the sign of the Spread Eagle (the arms with which the poet was afterwards to seal his letters) John Milton was born on Friday, 9 December, 1608, "half an hour after 6 in the morning," as he has recorded in a Bible which is now preserved in the British Museum. He had an elder sister Anne, whose fatherless sons, Edward and John Phillips, were to be his first pupils and his biographers. He had also a brother, seven years younger than himself, who was to have a successful legal career, survive his elder brother by nineteen years, and be knighted as Sir Christopher by James II.

"My father," says Milton, "destined me from a child to the pursuits of literature." No father could have taken more pains to provide for a son's education. Before going to St. Paul's School at the age of twelve, the child Milton had tutors at home, chief of whom was Thomas Young. In thanking Young for the gift of a Hebrew Bible, he writes: "Heaven knows that I regard you as a parent." It may well be that his tutor implanted in him, as well as a knowledge of the classics, a distrust of bishops. Young's father, a Scottish minister, had signed the petition of 1606 against the introduction of episcopacy into Scotland. Young himself was ordained in the English Church and held a benefice for twenty-seven years, but, when the Presbyterian cause was forging ahead on the eve of the Civil War, he was a leading spirit in the movement and his former pupil came to his defence.

A portrait of Milton at the age of ten, attributed to Cornelius Janssen, who came from Amsterdam that year and settled in Black Friars, shows an intelligent and serious face with auburn hair parted right and left; he has a striped doublet tightly fitting with many little buttons and a beautiful lace collar; his mother, as well as his father, was evidently proud of him. Some have supposed that Milton depicts his own childhood when he makes Christ tell of Himself in *Paradise Regained* (I, 201):

When I was yet a child, no childish play
To me was pleasing, all my mind was set

Serious to learn and know, and thence to do
What might be publick good; my self I thought
Born to that end, born to promote all truth,
All righteous things.

It may be noted that such recreations as Milton recommends for children in his treatise *On Education* are of a rather severe kind, "that they may despise and scorn all their childish and ill-taught qualities." At Cambridge, too, Milton had nothing but contempt for most of his fellow-students' amusements.

Milton was fortunate in spending five years in a famous London school. Its High Master, Alexander Gill, had succeeded another great schoolmaster, Richard Mulcaster, twelve years before Milton entered the school. Anthony Wood says of Gill that "many noted persons in church and state did esteem it the greatest of their happiness that they had been educated under him." He was not only an orthodox divine and a noted lutenist, but he had also a familiar knowledge of the Elizabethan poets, especially Spenser, the one of all his predecessors whom Milton most affected. Gill's son, also Alexander, was under-usher of St. Paul's, and Milton exchanged letters and verses with him for many years after leaving school; indeed, he tells Gill how greatly he misses his talk even at Cambridge, where "there are only two or three" whose talk does not quickly disappoint him.

From early years the boy Milton was only too ardent a scholar. He says of himself:

My appetite for knowledge was so voracious that, from twelve years of age, I hardly ever left my studies or went to bed before midnight. This primarily led to my loss of sight. My eyes were naturally weak and I was subject to frequent head-aches; which, however, could not chill the ardour of my curiosity or retard the progress of my improvement. (B., I, 254.)

Christopher Milton told Aubrey that "his father ordered ye mayde to sitt-up for" Master John, but it would have been a kinder act to send him to bed. Instead, his father with only too much encouragement pressed his son to the study, not only of the classics, but of Hebrew, French and Italian, besides some initiation into "the sciences." At the age of thirty-three Milton expressed his gratitude for having had "for my first years, by the ceaseless diligence and care of my father (whom God recompense!), been exercised to the tongues and some sciences, as my age would suffer, by sundry masters and teachers, both at home and at the schools" (B., II, 477).

At school Milton made the best friend among his contemporaries that he ever made. Charles Diodati, son of an Italian doctor, settled in London, and of an English mother, encouraged Milton's literary interests. For many years they corresponded freely and affectionately. "You shall be the critic to whom I shall recite my poems," Milton writes to Diodati, and again: "All my plans and dreams I was keeping to lay before you." Diodati's death at the age of thirty after a few years' practice as a physician was a severe loss to Milton, who only heard the particulars after his return from Italy and poured out his grief in the most beautiful of his Latin poems, *Epitaphium Damonis*. It was a far more personal grief than was shown in *Lycidas*. "Who now," he asks, "will teach me to lighten consuming cares and beguile the long nights with sweet converse? Who will renew for me your blandishments and laughter, your sallies and cultured graces?" It was, indeed, regrettable that Milton, only to self-sufficient and over-serious, should lose the one friend of equal years whose judgment he valued.

Soon after entering his seventeenth year Milton was admitted on 12 February, 1625, to Christ's College, Cambridge, and was to keep every term till he took his M.A. degree on 3 July, 1632. In Wordsworth's undergraduate days a friend of his was living "in the very room Honoured by Milton's name," on the north side of the First Court, and Wordsworth relates in *The Prelude* how at a festive gathering in that room they toasted the elder poet's memory and for once in his life he drank

> till my brain reel'd,
> Never so clouded by the fumes of wine
> Before that hour, or since.

Aubrey tells of Milton that "His widowe has his picture drawne, very well & like, when a Cambridge schollar." Soon after Mrs. Milton's death in 1727 the picture was bought by Mr. Speaker Onslow, and it remained in the Onslow family till it was sold in 1828, since which date it cannot be traced; but fortunately in 1792 the Speaker's son, Lord Onslow, had allowed his friend, Lord Harcourt, to have a faithful copy made by Benjamin van der Gucht. George Vertue and others made engravings of the Onslow picture. The light brown hair falling to the shoulders resembles the description of Adam in *Paradise Lost* (IV, 301), as Dr. Johnson remarked. The hair and the handsome and fresh complexion might well confirm Aubrey's suggestion that it was because he was "so faire" that they called him the Lady of Christ's. When Milton addressed his fellow-students in his *Vacation Exercise* in his twentieth year he rebuts the idea that he owes his nickname to any lack of virility, though he allows that it is not his way to toss off bumpers like a prize-fighter, nor are his hands grown horny from driving the plough. Throughout life he was conscious of his handsome face and his erect and manly gait. "His harmonicall and ingeniose soule," says Aubrey, "did lodge in a beautifull & well proportioned body," and he quotes Ovid's line—"In the whole of his body there was nowhere a blemish." When, some twenty years after he went to Cambridge, he was grossly attacked by a foreign controversialist as being mis-shapen, and disfigured by blindness, so that "there cannot be a more spare, shrivelled, and bloodless form," he hotly denied that he was undersized or pallid:

> I was strong and capable enough in my Youth to handle my Weapon and to exercise daily fencing; so that wearing a Sword by my side, as I usually did, I thought myself a match for those that were much stronger. . . . My Countenance, than which he says there's nothing paler, is still of a Color so contrary to wan and bloodless, that, though I am above forty, any body would think me ten years younger. (B., I, 235.)

Very much later in life he is remembered by his daughter Deborah as being "a little red in the cheeks." It was a consolation to him that the blindness which descended upon him when he was about forty-three was not disfiguring; his eyes, he says, are "yet to all outward appearance so sound, so clear, and free from the least spot, as theirs who see furthest; and herein only, in spite of my self, I am a Deceiver" (ibid.).

A certain natural aloofness and a consciousness of intellectual distinction made him at first none too popular with his fellows, and he did not conceal his contempt for their habits and pastimes. Nor was the old-fashioned curriculum which obtained in the university much to his mind, with its emphasis upon metaphysics, for which he had no liking, and its disregard of the new Baconian principles. He resented being required to compose Latin theses on scholastic subtleties which seemed to him remote from the real world. He did not have the good fortune to be taught by Joseph Meade, the most distinguished of the Fellows of Christ's, who was accustomed to ask his pupils, *"Quid dubitas?* What doubts have you met in your studies to-day?", and who said, "I cannot believe that truth can be prejudiced by the discovery of truth." There was a sad lack of sympathy between the independent-minded, argumentative youth and the Laudian churchman who was first assigned to Milton as tutor, and for some act of insubordination he was sent down for part of one term. In a Latin poem to Diodati he affects to make light of his short rustication: "How unfit is such a place for the worshippers of Phoebus! I have no mind to endure a rigid tutor's threats." The college authorities appear to have taken no severe view of his recalcitrance, as they assigned him, on his return, to another tutor. The incident would have mattered little if his opponents had not made a mountain of it sixteen years later. He was well able to repudiate their statement that he had been ejected in disgrace and obliged to flee to Italy. Their "commodious lie," he says,

hath given me an apt occasion to acknowledge publicly, with all grateful mind, that more than ordinary favour and respect, which I found above any of my equals at the hands of those courteous and learned men, the Fellows of that College wherein I spent some years: who at my parting, after I had taken two degrees . . . signified many ways how much better it would content them that I would stay; as by many Letters full of kindness and loving respect, both before that time, and long after, I was assured of their singular good affection towards me (B., III, 111).

In spite of the criticisms which Milton passed upon Cambridge studies, both at the time and, in still severer terms, later in life, it is probable that he gained more than most poets have done from a university training. His accurate and well-grounded knowledge of the classic and his aptness at composing in Latin woud serve him well both as poet and as Latin Secretary to the Council. He allows that his education had trained his literary sense:

> For this good hap I had from a careful education to be inured and seasoned betimes with the best and elegantest authors of the learned tongues, and thereto brought an ear that could measure a just cadence, and scan without articulating: rather nice and humorous in what was tolerable, than patient to read every drawling versifier. (B., III, 140.)

It appears from what he has said that, if he had desired to continue an academic career, he might have been elected to a fellowship in his own college, but, apart from his dissatisfaction with Cambridge curricula, his mind was clearly set on devoting all his powers to the sole purpose of writing poetry that should live.

Already he had begun to try his wings, and any one who was a less severe critic than Milton himself might well have been satisfied with what he had written before he left Cambridge in his twenty-fifth year, though nothing of his was yet in print except the epitaph on Shakespeare, written in 1630, which appeared anonymously in the second folio of 1632. In the *Vacation Exercise* the stripling of nineteen dared to announce to his probably incredulous fellow-students his project of writing on a theme as vast and daring as that of *Paradise Lost*:

> Such where the deep transported mind may soare
> Above the wheeling poles, and at Heav'ns dore

Look in, and see each blissful Deitie
How he before the thunderous throne doth lie,
Listening to what unshorn *Apollo* sings
To th' touch of golden wires.

If such a theme was already his aim, he would indeed need longer years of preparation, and would regard all smaller compositions of his as mere preludes to the great work. Yet those compositions included the ode "On the Morning of Christ's Nativity," which he wrote at the Christmas-tide of 1629 when he had just come of age. This ode foreshadows the poetry of *Paradise Lost*; already we hear the sonorous Miltonic line, especially in the Alexandrine which ends the opening stanzas as well as each verse of the Hymn that follows. He has not yet quite broken with conceits of "our late fantasticks," as he had named them, and there are other indications of his being still at the stage when he imitates Spenser and the Fletchers. With his remarkable power of self-criticism, even two years after writing the Nativity ode he shows himself conscious, in the sonnet on his ending his twenty-third year, that he still lacks "inward ripeness," and, in sending the sonnet to a friend who was concerned at his "tardy moving" towards the goal, he wisely defends himself as "not taking thought of being late, so it give advantage to be more fit."

Chapter 3

In a Buckinghamshire Village

IN THE YEAR that Milton left Cambridge his father had retired with a competency to the Buckinghamshire village of Horton, near Slough, and here the poet was to spend the next five years in studious retirement. No poet has ever prepared himself with more thoroughness and patience for his life's work than Milton, and no poet has been blest with a more understanding and patient father. It is evident from *Ad Patrem* that even this wise father was not easily reconciled to the idea of his gifted son entering no profession after seven years at the university. The first choice was ordination, which in that age was a usual background for those who intended to follow the pursuits of learning and literature. To the service of the Church, Milton told the world in *The Reason of Church Government* (1642), "by the intentions of my parents and friends I was destined of a child, and in mine own resolutions," and as late as his twenty-fifth year he had not wholly dismissed the notion, though he was for postponing it. But he had been alienated by what he saw of future ordinands at Cambridge, and growing years made him more than ever distrustful of the prelates, among whom Laud, though not yet archbishop, was already the dominating influence. Looking back at the age of thirty-three, and perhaps exaggerating what he had thought nine years earlier, he deemed that "tyranny had invaded the Church" and that "he who would take Orders must subscribe slave" (B., II, 482).

There need be no regret at his abandoning a profession which would never have suited him; his rebellious spirit would have brooked no control, whether of the Anglican, the Presbyterian or any other ecclesiastical authorities. His father's second choice for him was his own profession of the law, but the son thankfully allows that he was spared from any undue pressure, nor was the mere idea of making money put before him. Instead, he was suffered to spend the five

25

years at Horton in quiet and study, storing his mind and deepening his knowledge. "On my father's estate," he says, "I enjoyed an interval of uninterrupted leisure, which I entirely devoted to the perusal of the Greek and Latin classics; though I occasionally visited the metropolis, either for the sake of purchasing books, or of learning something new in mathematics or in music, in which I at that time found a source of pleasure and amusement" (B., I, 255). His studies included as well Italian literature and some history and philosophy.

He made also some progress in the composition of poetry, though the output is small compared with what other poets have produced before reaching the age of thirty. The two companion-pictures, *L'Allegro* and *Il Penseroso,* perhaps belong to the Horton years, but it is as likely that they were written at Cambridge. Milton's dextrous handling of the octosyllabic line was immediately successful, and the charm of these early poems and of *Lycidas* he would never surpass; many readers who fail to be captured by the great epic have loved these works of Milton's early manhood, which have indeed deserved their admiration, however their author might disparage them. In September 1637, three years after writing *Comus,* and shortly before writing *Lycidas,* he tells Diodati that he is meditating, with Heaven's help, "an immortality of fame," yet so far "I am letting my wings grow and preparing to fly; but my Pegasus has not yet feathers enough to soar aloft in the fields of air." Before writing *Comus* he had contributed three songs, including "Nymphs and Shepherds," and a poetic speech for the Genius of the Woods, to an entertainment under the title *Arcades* (The Arcadians), presented before the old Countess Dowager of Derby at Harefield House, near Uxbridge. This engagement probably led to his being invited by Henry Lawes, the Court musician, to assist him in a masque to be performed by the Earl of Bridgewater's children and their tutor, Lawes himself, at Ludlow Castle on the night of Michaelmas 1634. In *Paradise Lost* (IV, 767) Milton denounced "Court Amours, Mixt Dance, or wanton Mask," which he probably associated with the licentious court of Charles II, but at the age of twenty-six he saw no reason to decline his friend's offer, though he would fulfil the engagement in his own way.

A fashionable masque was an opportunity for pageantry, dress and scenery, combined with music and dance and poetry. Little more was expected from the poet in this mixed entertainment than a few lyrics and connecting poetic passages. The young Milton, however, was minded to give a libretto as long as a Greek play and to make every line as beautifully wrought as he could make it. With the high seriousness which he had already shown in the Cambridge years he chose for his theme the magical power of virginity. He was almost too successful in portraying the reveller Comus, as he was afterwards in depicting Satan, but Comus, for all the lovely language which the poet puts in his mouth, is moved in spite of himself by the innocence that arms the Lady, and exclaims, "Sure somthing holy lodges in that brest" (l. 246).

Three years later, Lawes published *A Maske,* without his own music or any allusion to it, and dedicated the work to Lord Bridgewater's eldest son. It is anonymous and "not openly acknowledg'd by the Author," but it brought Milton his earliest known appreciation from a man of letters. He had recently made the acquaintance of his neigbour Sir Henry Wotton, who after a career as ambassador at Venice had become Provost of Eton and entered holy orders. The author of "You meaner beauties of the Night" was a discerning judge, and on receiving from Milton a copy of *A Maske* he wrote: "I should much commend the Tragical part, if the Lyrical did not ravish me with a certain Dorique delicacy in your Songs and Odes, wherunto I must plainly confess to have seen yet nothing parallel in our Language." Wotton had, indeed, received a copy "som good while before" and viewed it "with singular delight," but it was only now that Milton had told him, "how modestly soever," that he was its author.

In the following year, 1638, the initials J. M. appeared at the foot of a poem entitled *Lycidas* in a little Cambridge volume commemorating the early death of Edward King, Fellow of Christ's, who was drowned on 10 August, 1637, while on his way to Ireland. King entered Christ's two years after Milton, and there is no reason to suppose that the two young men had had any close intimacy with one another. The sense of personal loss in *Lycidas* is not conspicuous; it is rather a lament on the death of the young with unfulfilled promise, and for that reason not the less welcome, as there is no theme that continues to tax the human heart more sorely. The sheer beauty of *Lycidas*, as of *Adonais*, does more to reconcile us than any details peculiar to Edward King or John Keats could have done. And if Milton does not forget himself in the elegy, neither did Wordsworth when he sang of "Chatterton, the marvellous Boy" and "Of Him who walked in glory and in joy Following his plough, along the mountain-side." *Lycidas* owes much to the pastoral elegists of antiquity and of the Elizabethan age, but perhaps surpasses them all; yet its author even now can speak of the myrtleberries he offers as "harsh and crude," plucked before their ripeness. And this modest disclaimer comes from one who can write such lines as these:

Bring the rathe Primrose that forsaken dies,
The tufted Crow-toe, and pale Gessamine,
The white Pink, and the Pansie freakt with jeat,
The glowing Violet.
The Musk-rose, and the well attir'd Woodbine.
With Cowslips wan that hang the pensive hed,
And every flower that sad embroidery wears:
Bid *Amaranthus* all his beauty shed,
And Daffadillies fill their cups with tears,
To strew the Laureat Herse where *Lycid* lies.

There is only one passage in *Lycidas* that flecks its perfection; it is described in the heading given to the poem in 1645 where the author "by occasion foretels the ruine of our corrupted Clergy then in their height." It is not the justice or injustice of St. Peter's wholesale denunciation of the clergy that makes its propriety here questionable. It is, doubtless, a sincere expression of that ruthless spirit of Milton which made him three years later end his treatise *Of Reformation* with a prayer that the bishops "after a shameful end in this life (which God grant them,) shall be thrown down eternally into the darkest and deepest gulf of hell" (B., II, 419). It is not the uncharitable judgment in *Lycidas* that matters, as out of it Milton has made fine and effective poetry which we could ill spare, but it argues a curious insensitiveness to include this bitter indictment of the Church in an elegy upon a gifted young man who was intending to devote his life to its ministry.

Chapter 4

Milton in Italy

ALTHOUGH MILTON had given clear proof of his poetic ability before he was thirty, he did not think his preparation complete enough to equip him for writing an immortal work. After more than five years at Horton he may have exhausted the stimulus which its country scenes and its opportunities for private study afforded him. His mother had recently died, and his indulgent father found the means for his son to go abroad, attended by a man-servant, in April 1638. Henry Lawes procured him a passport, and the old Provost of Eton furnished him with letters of introduction. It is creditable to the old aristocratic order that this young man of inconspicuous birth and barely known yet as a poet was helped by his countrymen of high rank to be received in France and Italy with the greatest courtesy. The ambassador in Paris, Lord Scudamore, a disciple of Laud, received him "most courteously" and sent him with a card of introduction to call on the great Dutch scholar, Hugo Grotius, at that time ambassador from the Queen of Sweden. On leaving Paris Scudamore gave him letters to the English merchants on his route, and, taking ship from Nice to Genoa, Milton passed through Leghorn and Pisa to Florence.

At Florence he received a friendly welcome from its men of letters, who invited him to their Academies or literary societies. They praised his Latin poems and indited poems in his honour, which he proudly prefixed to his own Latin poems when he published them in 1645. They envied him the philosophic freedom which England was reputed to enjoy, and he resolved then and there that his country should be made better deserving of that reputation when it was secured from "the prelatical yoke." Florence was also for ever memorable to him because, either on this first visit or on his return there the next year, he went to see Galileo, now in his seventy-fifth year, blind and living under house-arrest on the left bank of the Arno. Milton describes him as "a prisoner to the Inquisition, for thinking in astronomy otherwise than the Franciscan and Dominican licensers thought" (B., II, 82). Galileo was to be the only contemporary whom Milton would name in *Paradise Lost*—"the Tuscan Artist" who viewed the moon's orb through his optic glass "at Ev'ning from the top of Fesole" (P.L., I, 287, and V, 262).

From Florence he went on to Rome, where also he received "the most friendly attentions." He was shown the manuscript treasures of the Vatican by its librarian. He was invited to "a grand musical entertainment" at the palace of the illustrious Cardinal Francesco Barberini, who "waited for me at the door, sought me out among the crowd, took me by the hand, and introduced me into the palace with every mark of the most flattering distinction" (B., III, 499). It was probably at this concert that he heard Leonora Baroni sing, which moved him to write three Latin epigrams in her honour. The English College at Rome, the famous seminary for English-speaking priests, still has "Johannes Milton, Anglus" recorded in its visitors' book.

After two months in Rome Milton proceeded to Naples, where he was introduced "by a certain hermit, with whom I had travelled from Rome, to Giovanni Battista Manso, Marquis of Villa, a nobleman of distinguished rank and authority, to whom Torquato Tasso, the illustrious poet, inscribed his book *On Friendship*. During my stay, he gave me singular proofs of his regard: he himself conducted me round the city and to the palace of the viceroy; and more than once paid me a visit at my lodgings" (B., I, 256). Manso even apologized for not doing more, because his guest "had spoken with so little reserve on matters of religion." This is corroborated by Manso's distich on Milton, in which he says that if Englishman's religion had matched his intellect, the beauty of his person and his charming manners, he would be not an Angle but an Angel. Sir Henry Wotton had pressed on Milton the need for reticence on religious matters, by which, like Wotton himself when he resided in Italy, he could carry himself securely "without offence of others or of mine own conscience." According to his own account, Milton made it a rule not to begin any conversation on religion, "but if any questions were put to me concerning my faith, to declare it without any reserve or fear," and, on his second visit to Rome, " I again openly defended, as I had done before, the orthodox religion in the very metropolis of the Pontiff." Italy seems to have been more tolerant of his outspoken heresy than he was to be, in his writings at least, of popery and prelacy.

While still in Naples, towards the close of 1638, and meditating the extension of his tour to Sicily and Greece, Milton received news of the troubles brewing between King Charles and his subjects. He curtailed his programme, "for I thought it base to be travelling at my ease abroad, even for the benefit of my mind, while my fellow-citizens were fighting for liberty at home" (B.,I, 256). He made, however, a leisurely return from Naples, spending two months at Rome, another two at Florence, a month at Venice, and making visits to other famous cities on his way to Geneva, where also he stayed some time. He was back in England, after an absence of a year and a quarter, by the end of July 1639.

Chapter 5

Milton, Educator and Pamphleteer

ON HIS RETURN home Milton settled in London and received into his house his sister's two fatherless boys, Edward and John Phillips, as his pupils. To these he added after a while a few other boys specially commended to him, including the Earl of Barrimore and an Essex baronet. Milton's treatise *On Education* (1644) throws much light on his aims and methods. He had evidently in mind boys of social standing who should be trained to take their part in national life. He describes a generous education as "that which fits a man to perform justly, skilfully, and magnanimously all the offices, both private and public, of peace and war" (B., III, 467). His nephew Edward records that in a year's time the brothers, aged ten and nine, were made "capable of interpreting a Latin authour at sight & within 3 years they went through y° best of Latin & Greec Poetts."

Like Plato, Milton did not overlook the training of the body, but this should be done less through idle pastimes than through fencing, wrestling and "military motions." In "the interim of unsweating themselves" they could relax and soften their spirits with "the solemn and divine harmonies of Musick, heard or learnt." And this rather exacting taskmaster recognized as clearly as Wordsworth the call of Nature bidding the wise to "quit their books"; "when the air is calm and pleasant, it were an injury and sullenness against nature not to go out and see her riches, and partake in her rejoycing with Heaven and Earth" (B., III, 477). Here speaks the author of *L'Allegro* and *Il Penseroso* as surely as elsewhere we note the intellectual ardour of the Renaissance scholar. There is also the religious emphasis of the future author of *Paradise Lost* when the educator writes that "the end of learning is to repair the ruins of our first parents by regaining to know God aright, and out of that knowledge to love him, to imitate him, to be like him, as we may the nearest by possessing our souls of true virtue, which being united to the heavenly grace of faith

35

makes up the highest perfection" (B., III, 464). As his nephew
tells, he expounded the Greek Testament to them on Sundays,
took them through the Pentateuch in Hebrew, and even introduced them to the Targum and to some chapters of St.
Matthew's Gospel in Syriac.

This full programme did not deter Milton from prosecuting
his own studies and from a considerable amount of writing.
This writing, however, was not of poetry, which fell into almost complete abeyance for nearly twenty years, but on
public affairs. "For some few years yet," he wrote, he must
"go on trust" with the reader for the fulfilment of his promise
of writing a great poem, and meanwhile devote his powers to
the cause of liberty. "When God commands to take the
trumpet," he cannot refuse, however much it cost him to
desert his peaceful studies and "to embark in a troubled sea
of noises and hoarse disputes," to abandon poetry for "the
cool element of prose," in which, he said, he had but the use
of his left hand. He recalled the lament of Jeremiah: "Wo is
me, my mother, that thou hast borne me, a man of strife and
contention"; but "if God by his secretary Conscience enjoin
it, it were sad for me if I should draw back; for me especially,
now when all men offer their aid to help, ease, and lighten the
difficult labours of the Church" (B., II, 482).

It is significant that Milton's first treatises deal with the
ecclesiastical rather than with the directly political issues of
the time. Like many others on both sides, he believed that the
religious question was at the heart of the great civil contention. King Charles's conflict with his Scots subjects arose out
of the attempt to impose episcopacy and liturgy upon them,
and when at last he was driven to summon a parliament after
an interval of eleven years it was because he needed money
for what was nicknamed the Bishops' War and which Milton
contemptuously called making "a national war of a surplice-
brabble." When the Long Parliament met, a few months after
the abortive Short Parliament, on 3 November, 1640, it proceeded at once to impeach and commit to the Tower both
Strafford and Laud. A month after the opening, a member for
the City of London presented a petition for the abolition of
episcopacy "with all its dependencies, roots and branches."
Even Sir Benjamin Rudyard, who was for a limited episco-

pacy, said: "Let Religion be our *primum quaerite,* for all things else are but etceteras to it."

During the next few months the church question absorbed more attention than the political, perhaps because the execution of Strafford on 12 May, 1641, seemed to end for good and all the system of "thorough." The issue between the abolition and the drastic limitation of episcopacy still hung in the balance when Milton joined the fray with a series of anonymous pamphlets supporting the Root and Branch reformers. With grim satisfaction he could see the prophecy of *Lycidas* already near fulfilment:

> But that two-handed engine at the door
> Stands ready to smite once, and smite no more.

He believed that religious liberty and a more thorough reformation were incompatible with the retention of episcopacy. He had at this time no such conviction that political liberty was incompatible with the retention of monarchy. So far from accepting James I's dictum "No bishop, no king," he maintained in his first treatise, *Of Reformation in England,* that the English monarchy had had no worse counsellors throughout its history than the bishops.

There was a further and more personal reason that brought Milton into the field. His old tutor, Thomas Young, for the last twelve years Vicar of Stowmarket, was the leader of a group of five beneficed clergymen of Puritan mind who produced an answer to Bishop Hall's *Humble Remonstrance to the High Court of Parliament* which was a temperate defence of a limited episcopacy. Their joint production, *An Answer to An Humble Remonstrance* (March, 1641) is described on the title-page as "Written by Smectymnuus," a name formed from the initials of the five authors. This heavy-going treatise provoked a host of others, in support or in attack, and there was a clear need for something more brightly written on the Puritan side. Milton's treatise begins heavily enough; the average length of its first four sentences is twenty-two lines each, but soon we meet with some of the gibes which enliven his pamphleteering, as, for instances, when he mocks at the bishops in their mitres "and gewgaws fetched from Aaron's old wardrobe or the flamens' vestry." He makes quick work of his opponents' appeal to antiquity and refuses to see any sufficient ground for following the practices whether of the primitive church, in which he detects much corruption, or of the sixteenth-century English reformers who showed more timidity than the continental. His appeal is the typically Puritan one to Scripture only:

> But I trust they for whom God hath reserved the honour of reforming this Church will easily perceive their adversaries' drift in thus calling for Antiquity. They fear the plain field of the Scriptures; the chase is too hot; they seek the dark, the bushy, the tangled forest; they would imbosk. They feel themselves strook in the transparent streams of divine truth; they would plunge and tumble and think to lie hid in the foul weeds and muddy waters where no plummet can reach the bottom. But let them beat themselves like whales, and spend their oil, till they be dredged ashore. (B., II, 389.)

Our interest to-day can hardly be engaged in this controversy with its partisanship and interchange of scurrilities, but we should still assent to Milton's plea that it boded ill for "our dear mother England" when so many of her most conscientious sons sought refuge across "the wide ocean" from their "insufferable grievances at home" (B., II, 399). We might also regret with him the isolation of the English Church from "our neighbour reformed sister-churches."

Two further anonymous treatises of Milton's followed in the summer of 1641. The author adopts the Presbyterian doctrine that "bishop and presbyter were anciently one," not separate orders. He expresses his contempt for "that indigested heap and fry of authors which they call antiquity": "Whatsoever time, or the heedless hand of blind chance, hath drawn down from of old to this present, in her huge drag-net, whether fish or sea-weed, shells or shrubs, unpicked, unchosen, those are the Fathers" (B., II, 422). He would fain recall the people of God "from this vain foraging after straw" to the sole standard of the Gospel.

There is also much contempt for the Prayer Book, "a patched missal," "the old riff-raff of Sarum," without any recognition of the beauty and dignity of its language. If the Remonstrant tries to make a case for a liturgy, he is answered that the variety of "kitchen physic" should teach him better; there is, indeed, "an order of breakfast, dinner, and supper," but "Is a man therefore bound in the morning to poached eggs and vinegar, or at noon to brawn or beef, or at night to fresh salmon and French kickshoes?" It is remarkable that the writer can pass from such cheap language to a passage of great dignity in which he announces the dawn of a purer reformation in this present age "which is to us an age of ages wherein God is manifestly come down among us, to do some remarkable good to our church or state" (B., III, 69).

> Every one can say, that now certainly thou hast visited this land, and hast not forgotten the utmost corners of the earth, in a time when men had thought that thou *wast* gone up from us to the farthest end of the heavens, and hadst left to do marvellously among the sons of these last ages. O perfect and accomplish thy glorious acts! for men may leave their works unfinished, but thou art a God, thy nature is perfection. (B., III, 71.)

In such an apocalyptic outburst the pamphleteer becomes the prophet.

After a silence of more than six months Milton produced a graver and more scholarly work under his own name, *The Reason of Church Government urg'd against Prelaty* (February, 1642). In a discussion of the relations of Church and State it is argued that church discipline should be spiritual only, unsupported by the secular arm. Milton desires to see episcopacy replaced by a presbyterian system, more or less on the Scots model. He is not greatly concerned that the new liberty should at first result in a proliferation of sects and schisms; "it best beseems our Christian courage to think they are but as the throes and pangs that go before the birth of reformation, and that the work itself is now in doing" (B., II, 469). This was a braver acceptance of religious diversity than the Presbyterians were willing to tolerate, as Milton was soon to discover, when, in his sonnet "On the new Forcers of Conscience under the Long Parliament," he declared:

New Presbyter is but old Priest writ large.

Of more lasting interest than the argument of *The Reason of Church Government* is the autobiographical passage, extending over a dozen pages. When now for the first time Milton published a treatise under his own name, he was entitled to state his credentials, all the more because the character of the anonymous writer had been traduced. Milton maintains that a man's "wise and true valuation of himself" is "a requisite and high point of Christianity," and he was always fully conscious of his intellectual and moral superiority to other men. He believed himself endowed with such abilities as would one day enable him to write poetry which will commemorate for ever the achievements of "a great people." With less strict appropriateness to a controversial pamphlet, but with that characteristic absorption in his own plans which makes him ready to believe that they are also of national concern, he proceeds to discuss whether epic, ode, or drama is best fitted to be the form of what he shall hereafter write "doctrinal and exemplary to a nation" (B., II, 479).

A month later Milton published a hastily written treatise called *An Apology for Smectymnuus*, which is a defence as much of himself as of the Puritan tractarians. He allows that it is hard "when a man meets with a fool to keep his tongue from folly," and he does not always escape the temptation. An instance may be given of the degree in which even his literary sense deserts him in his angry assault on the Anglican liturgy. The beautiful psalm, *Levavi oculos,* appointed for the service of the Churching of Women, includes the verses: "Behold, he that keepeth Israel shall neither slumber nor sleep. The Lord himself is thy keeper, . . . so that the sun shall not burn thee by day, neither the moon by night." This choice leads Milton to protest that the mother is bidden to give thanks "for her delivery from Sunburning and Moonblasting, as if she had been travailing, not in her bed, but in the deserts of Arabia" (B., III, 158).

Yet this treatise, too, is interesting for its long autobiographical passages. His anonymous opponents—Bishop Hall, then a prisoner in the Tower, and his son—had sought to destroy Milton's character by reflections on his having been "vomited out" of Cambridge and then residing in "a suburb sink," where he restored to play-houses and brothels. This is more than a return for Milton's previous description of the bishop as "a belly-God, proud and covetous," "a false prophet," with other opprobrious names. Milton tells the true story of his Cambridge life and dilates upon the chastity of mind and body which he has preserved at every stage of his life. For the author of *Comus* chastity was one of the most cherished virtues and as obligatory for men as for women. Moreover, the regards it as peculiarly requisite for one who aspires to write great poetry:

> He who would not be frustrate of his hope to write well hereafter in laudable things, ought himself to be a true Poem; that is, a composition and pattern of the best and honourablest things; not presuming to sing high praises of heroic men or famous cities, unless he have in himself the experience and the practice of all that which is praiseworthy. (B., III, 118.)

Milton knew that such a work as he intended was "not to be raised from the heat of youth or the vapours of wine," nor could it be "obtained by the invocation of Dame Memory and her Siren daughters, but by devout prayer to that eternal Spirit, who can enrich with all utterance and knowledge, and sends out his Seraphim with the hallowed fire of his altar to touch and purify the lips of whom he pleases" (B., II, 481). He dedicated himself and all his abilities to his high mission with as much conscious deliberation as the young Isaiah whose words he here echoes. Wordsworth, too, who so closely resembles Milton at many points, consecrated himself to his work as poet on that morning when, after passing a night "in dancing, gaiety and mirth," he made his way home in the early hours across the Cumbrian hills:

> Magnificent
> The morning rose, in memorable pomp,
> Glorious as e'er I had beheld—in front,
> The sea lay laughing at a distance; near,
> The solid mountains shone, bright as the clouds,
> Grain-tinctured, drenched in empyrean light;
> And in the meadows and the lower grounds

Was all the sweetness of a common dawn—
Dews, vapours, and the melody of birds,
And labourers going forth to till the fields.
Ah! need I say, dear Friend! that to the brim
My heart was full; I made no vows, but vows
Were then made for me; bond unknown to me
Was given, that I should be, else sinning greatly,
A dedicated Spirit.

Chapter 6

Milton's Marriage and the Divorce Treatises

MEANWHILE throughout the year 1642, ever since the king's vain attempt to arrest the five members in the House of Commons on 4 January, and his leaving London six days after, the tension between king and parliament was rapidly growing, and, in the eyes of the most observant, civil war was imminent. Already from April both sides began to levy forces, the king by appointing commissions of array, the parliament through the lords-lieutenants. When Charles set up his standard at Nottingham on 22 August it was taken to be the signal that a state of war had begun.

It has excited some surprise that Milton did not bear arms. By his own account he was a good fencer, and in his treatise *On Education* he recommended military exercises for the young. In his answer to the slanderous charge of his living dissolutely in London he had already, five months before the outbreak of war, described his day as made up not only of assiduous study but also of hardy exercise that he might be fit to serve "the cause of religion and our country's liberty, when it shall require firm hearts in sound bodies to stand and cover their stations, rather than to see the ruin of our Protestation and the enforcement of a slavish life" (B., III, 113). It is, however, certain that he did not bear arms in the Civil War, as he defends himself against any charge of want of courage or zeal in the *Second Defence* in the following terms:

> For though I did not participate in the toils or dangers of the war, yet I was at the same time engaged in a service not less hazardous to myself and more beneficial to my fellow-citizens. . . . For since from my youth I was devoted to the pursuits of literature, and my mind had always been stronger than my body, I did not court the labours of a camp, in which any common person would have been of more service than myself, but resorted to that employment in which my exertions were likely to be of more avail. (B., I, 218.)

43

A further possible reason for Milton's not offering himself for military service in 1642 is that he had recently married a wife. It has commonly been supposed that his marriage was a year later, in the early summer of 1643, but almost from the beginning of the war Oxford was an important military centre for the royalists, and it would have been difficult for Milton to visit his future bride's home within five miles of that city. Our chief source of authority is his elder nephew Edward, who names no year for the coming of the bride and "some few of her nearest Relations" to Aldersgate Street, but he states that it was before the poet's father had gone there, which was not till after the taking of Reading by Lord Essex on 26 April, 1643. Edward Phillips was only a boy of twelve or thirteen at the time, living with his uncle, and he is writing some fifty years after the event, but this is his account:

About *Whitsuntide* it was, or a little after, that he took a Journey into the Country; no body about him certainly knowing the Reason, or that it was any more than a Journey of Recreation: after a Month's stay, home he returns a Married man, that went out a Batchelor; his wife being *Mary*, the Eldest Daughter of Mr. *Richard Powell*, then a Justice of Peace, of *Forrest-hil*, near *Shotover* in *Oxfordshire*; some few of her nearest Relations accompanying the Bride to her new Habitation; which by reason the Father nor any body else were yet come, was able to receive them.

Forest Hill was within a mile of Stanton St. John, where Milton's father was born, and father and son had had financial dealings with Richard Powell fifteen years before. It was a usual part of a scrivener's practice to advance loans. Powell and his wife were well-to-do, but he was constantly in money difficulties, and on 11 June, 1627, Richard Powell and William Hearne, a London goldsmith, had signed a deed by which they "acknowledge themselves to owe unto John Milton, then of the University of Cambridge, gentleman, son of John Milton, citizen and scrivener of London, the sum of £500."

Perhaps John Milton junior went to Forest Hill in the early

summer of 1642 to recover some part of the debt, now that civil war was brewing. Whatever cause took him there, he returned with a bride half his age, Mary Powell having been baptized on 24 January, 1626, and being now only sixteen and a half, and Milton being half-way through his thirty-fourth year, looking younger than his age but grave beyond his years. He was not unsusceptible to female beauty, as he had confessed in early poems and letters, but hitherto he had formed no definite attachment, and now that he was settled in London with two young nephews to live with him it was high time that he should take a wife. One of his early biographers remarks that "he was always in haste," and there was a dangerous precipitateness in this swift courtship and marriage before he had had time to discover much of his future wife's mind and character. For once Milton's usual control of his life by reason was disastrously remitted, and this bitter lesson he would heed for the rest of life and make it a principal theme of *Paradise Lost* and *Samson Agonistes*.

Disillusion descended at once upon the married couple. No sooner had the bride's relations returned home after some days' nuptial celebrations than she became homesick when she found herself left to the society of her austere and highly intellectual husband, who must again betake himself to his studies and to the education of his nephews. Edward Phillips says that Milton's young wife had been "used to a great House, and much Company and Joviality," and his brother John says that "she had bin bred in a family of plenty and freedom" and was not well pleased with her husband's "reserv'd manner of life." Aubrey, perhaps with less warrant than the Phillips brothers, says that she "oftentimes heard his Nephews beaten and cry." After she had "for a Month or thereabout led a Philosophical Life," as Edward describes it, she yielded to a pressing invitation to go on a visit to her parents, and Milton reluctantly consented on condition of her returning to him by Michaelmas. Michaelmas did not bring her, his subsequent letters were disregarded, and a messenger whom he sent was "dismissed with some contempt." The Powells were royalists, and the royalist control of Oxford and its neighbourhood must have made communications difficult. Mary shared her parents' attachment to church and king, and, as Aubrey remarks, "Two opinions doe not well on the same Boulster."

The husband's sense of frustration was naturally acute. It was a marriage and no marriage, and four years would pass before his wife returned to him. Meanwhile the legal tie which held him to one who was a wife in name only and who had deserted him offended both his self-esteem and his sense of justice. The earlier dating of the marriage spares us from the common view that he wrote the first Divorce treatise during his honeymoon; there is a lapse of almost exactly a year between Mary's leaving him and the publication of *The Doctrine and Discipline of Divorce* (August, 1643). The first edition did not bear the author's name, but in the second enlarged edition (February, 1644) he appended his name to the prefatory letter addressed to Parliament and the Assembly of Divines.

According to John Phillips, it had been "formerly" his uncle's opinion that a marriage which failed of "the purposes for which marriage was at first instituted" should be terminable by divorce to allow a of more suitable mating. It is improbable, however, that Milton would have publicly advocated divorce in four successive treatises if he had not had this unhappy experience. In the light of it he set himself to examine the true nature, as he conceived it, of the marriage tie. With his habitual concern for freedom, he saw the existing law as a fetter, and he would be the readier to criticize it because its regulation was traditionally a province of ecclesiastical authority. He still accepted the Scriptures as binding, but disputed the Church's interpretation of them. He claimed that his argument had the support of the Bible, though it sometimes involved his straining the plain sense of a text in a way which did not convince his readers then or since.

In the treatises Milton does not mention his own case, but he does cite desertion as a ground for divorce, and he keeps stressing incompatibility of temper as a principal ground. He is even indignant that the law provided for divorce where physical disability was proved, but gave no remedy for the release of those who were temperamentally irreconcilable.

It was not that he held a lax view of marriage, but that he had a more intimately personal conception of its nature, like Shakespeare's ideal of "the marriage of true minds," than the laws of any church or state could safeguard and enforce. He conceived of it, less as a means of satisfying natural desire and of propagating the race, than as the alleviation of man's solitariness. He quoted the old words of *Genesis*: "It is not good that the man should be alone: I will make him a help meet for him." He looked, above all, for "a fit conversing soul," because in the Divne intention "a meet and happy conversation is the chiefest and noblest end of marriage." But what if, instead, a man, even through his inexperience and misjudgment, "chances on a mute and spiritless mate"? Is there no way of remedying the mistake? "It is a less breach of wedlock to part with wise and quiet consent betimes, than still to soil and profane that mystery of joy and union with a polluting sadness and perpetual distemper" (B., III, 196). If there proves to be between the married pair "indisposition, unfitness, or contrariety of mind, arising from a cause in nature unchangeable, hindering and ever likely to hinder the main benefits of conjugal society, which are solace and peace," it is better that they should part than make a vain attempt "to fadge together and combine as they may, to their unspeakable wearisomeness and despair of all sociable delight in the ordinance which God establisht to that very end" (B., III, 181 and 185).

Milton objected to the idea of the indissolubility of marriage, except for the single cause of fornication; he regarded it as a merciless infliction, and urged that, by the Church insisting on "so sacramental" a view, "our Saviour's words touching divorce are as it were congealed into a stony rigour, inconsistent both with his doctrine and his office" (B., III, 182). He repelled the suggestion that he was lending any countenance to "licence, and levity, and unconsented breach of faith," but pleaded "that some conscionable and tender pity might be had of those who have unwarily, in a thing they never practised before, made themselves the bondmen of a luckless and helpless matrimony" (183).

He even maintains that those who had spent their youth chastely were more likely than the vicious to make mistakes in choosing a bride because of their inexperience of women. "The soberest and best governed men are least practised in these affairs; and who knows not that the bashful muteness of a virgin may ofttimes hide all the unliveliness and natural sloth which is really unfit for conversation?" (190). A man's generous mistake in "honouring the appearance of modesty, and hoping well of every social virtue under that veil" may lead him to choose a wife who is "to all other due conversation inaccessible, and to all the more estimable and superior purposes of matrimony useless and almost lifeless" (190). If, as is inevitable, Milton has Mary Powell in mind, he may have found her after marriage, not so much lively and frivolous as sullen and silent, wholly unable or making no effort to rise to the level of his philosophical and literary talk. He looked for more intellectual companionship from her than he had any right to expect with his slight previous knowledge of her. One of his opponents, in the war of pamphlets that sought to traverse Milton's view, came near the mark when, picking up a phrase which Milton had used, he wrote:

> It is true, if every man were of your breeding and capacity, there were some colour for this plea; for we believe you to count no woman to due conversation accessible as to you, except she can speak Hebrew, Greek, Latin and French, and dispute against the Canon Law as well as you, or at least be able to hold discourse with you. But other gentlemen of good quality are content with fewer and meaner endowments, as you know well enough.

Milton regarded the whole matter too much from the man's point of view; it is ultimately, he thinks, for the man alone to determine the woman's fitness or unfitness to continue as his wife, though he allows it to be better if the parting is by mutual consent. Mary Milton's continued absence from her husband entitled him to think that the separation was rather her wish than his. The superiority of man to woman is unquestioned by Milton, though he has the grace to allow that "it is no small glory to him that a creature so like him should be made subject to him." Once even he goes so far as to admit that there may be exceptional cases where a man may recognize his wife's superiority, "if she exceed her husband in prudence and dexterity, and he contentedly yield; for then a superior and more natural law comes in, that the wiser should govern the less wise, whether male or female" (B., III, 325). But normally the authority rests with the man. He fortifies his argument less from the New than from the Old Testament; he cites the Hebrew husband's right (Deuteronomy xxiv. I) to send away his wife with a bill of divorcement "because he hath found some unseemly thing in her," which he unjustifiably takes to include any moral or intellectual incompatibility. "Who can be ignorant," he asks, "that woman was created for man, and not man for woman?" (247).

Milton's was indeed a hard case, even though, as he knew in his heart, he had himself to blame for his momentary surrender to a physical attraction which blinded his judgment. If he was right in thinking that there was no chance of this marriage bringing him the fit companionship which he took to be the chief end of matrimony, it is not enough to say that no law can adequately provide for hard cases. As he did not accept the church's sacramental view of indissoluble marriage, he was entitled to ask if the civil law need any longer support that view, especially now that a new reformation was, he believed, in sight. He charged the church with making "imaginary and scarecrow sins." But if there was any hope of his persuading the Parliament, he was unduly sanguine in supposing that the Westminster Assembly of Divines, to whom also he addressed his appeal, would be any more ready to condone "moral" than doctrinal heresies. Geneva and the Presbyterians would take alarm as certainly as Rome and the Anglican bishops. And this he found to his cost.

An eminent divine of the Assembly, preaching before the Houses of Parliament in St. Margaret's, Westminster, on a solemn fast-day, 13 August, 1644, against things not to be tolerated, spoke of "a wicked book abroad and uncensored, though deserving to be burnt, whose Author hath been so impudent as to set his name to it and dedicate it to yourselves." Eleven days after this public denunciation the Stationers Company petitioned Parliament concerning the publication of unlicensed and unregistered pamphlets in defiance of the recent parliamentary Ordinance of 14 June, 1643, for the regulation of printing. The Stationers expressly mention the two editions of Milton's first Divorce treatise, neither of which bore the printer's name. Their petition, and a similar one later, had no serious effect, except that it moved Milton to interrupt the series of his Divorce pamphlets to take up the case against licensing in *Areopagitica*, the greatest of his prose writings, the discussion of which is postponed to the next chapter.

The three Divorce treatises which follow the first do not add to Milton's reputation. In spite of their length, he does not address himself to the practical difficulties, such as the interests of the children if any, the social disadvantages of instability of the married state, and, above all, the husband's advantage over the wife. The interpretation of Scriptural texts is often strained. Worst of all, he answers scurrility with scurrility, and wastes his strength on opponents unworthy of his steel, and sinks to their level. "I mean not to dispute philosophy with this pork, who never read any" (445). "But what should a man say more to a snout in this pickle? What language can be low and degenerate enough?" (453). Yet unfortunately Milton has much more to say to "this clod of an antagonist," till the reader is thankful when he reaches "a concluding taste" of his opponent's "jabberment in law, the flashiest and the fustiest that ever corrupted in such an unswilled hogshead" (459). "This most incogitant woodcock" is only too easy game for Milton's cudgelling.

While Milton was writing this series of polemical treatises he was engaged in teaching his nephews, with no wife to look after the household. He made a home for his father, who had been living with his younger son Christopher at Reading until Essex took that town in April 1643. Edward Phillips tells of "the Old Gentleman living wholly retired to his Rest and Devotion without the least trouble imaginable." There he lived under his elder son's roof until he died and on 15 March, 1647, was buried in the chancel of St. Giles's, Cripplegate, where the poet was to lie twenty-seven years later. Milton's affectionate devotion to his father throughout life is a pleasing trait in a character which was not conspicuously open to tenderness. Not that he was unsociable; his nephew Edward reports that his uncle in his bachelor days would allow himself an evening off once every three weeks or so to "keep a Gawdy-day" in the society of "some young Sparks of his acquaintance," especially two gentlemen of Gray's Inn, "the Beaus of those Times, but nothing near so bad as those now-a-days." In the four years of his wife's desertion he was not without female society. His "chief diversion," according to his nephew, was to spend an evening with his neighbours in Aldersgate, Captain Hobson, who bore arms in the parliamentary forces, and his wife Lady Margaret, "daughter to that good Earl," James Ley, Earl of Marlborough. "This Lady being a Woman of great Wit and Ingenuity had a particular Honour for him, and took much delight in his Company, as likewise her Husband, Captain Hobson, a very accomplish'd Gentleman." To the Lady Margaret one of Milton's most admired sonnets is addressed.

Edward Phillips, who, it must be remembered, was only about fifteen at the time he writes of, states that his uncle had "a design of Marrying one of Dr. Davis's Daughters, a very Handsome and Witty Gentlewoman," but that she was said to be "averse to this Motion," as well she might be, seeing that there was small chance of the marriage law being altered. John Phillips says that his uncle was actually "in treaty" for a marriage, but he does not give the lady's name. Edward suggests that the Powells got wind of this project, and that this was one of the reasons why Mary now sought means of reconciliation to her husband. The other reason which Edward gives is perhaps the more substantial—"the then declining State of the King's Cause." With the surrender of Oxford, where the Powells had been living since the war began, on Midsummer Day, 1646, their fortunes were at a low ebb, and they sought to rehabilitate them, at least for a time, by turning to the neglected husband. It was known to them that Milton was in the habit of visiting a relation of his in St. Martin's Le Grand Lane, and on one such occasion they contrived that he should be confronted with his wife. This is how Edward Phillips describes the event:

> One time above the rest, he making his usual visit, the Wife was ready in another Room, and on a sudden he was surprised to see one whom he thought to have never seen

more, making Submission and begging Pardon on her Knees before him; he might probably at first make some shew of aversion and rejection; but partly his own generous nature, more inclinable to Reconciliation than to perseverance in Anger and Revenge; and partly the strong intercession of Friends on both sides, soon brought him to an Act of Oblivion, and a firm League of Peace for the future.

We cannot but recognize something of the poet's painful memories of this scene in the beautiful passage in *Paradise Lost* which describes Eve's humble submission to her husband after she has eaten of the forbidden fruit, Adam's first impulsive denunciation of her and of the whole female sex, and his gradual melting when Eve "with Tears that ceas'd not flowing, And tresses all disorder'd, at his feet Fell humble" and owned that she was "sole cause to thee of all this woe":

> She ended weeping, and her lowlie plight,
> Immoveable till peace obtain'd from fault
> Acknowledg'd and deplor'd, in *Adam* wraught
> Commiseration; soon his heart relented
> Towards her, his life so late and sole delight,
> Now at his feet submissive in distress,
> Creature so faire his reconcilement seeking,
> His counsel whom she had displeas'd, his aide;
> As one disarm'd, his anger all he lost,
> And thus with peaceful words uprais'd her soon.

(X, 937).

Edward Phillips says of his uncle's previous mind that Mary's refusal to return to him in spite of his many messages to her "so incensed our Author, that he thought it would be dishonourable ever to receive her again, after such a repulse." For a man of proud spirit who had perhaps dismissed from his mind the possibility of reconciliation and who had over and over again expatiated on the thraldom of the existing marriage law, it was, doubtless, a difficult decision to make. His early biographers, including both his nephews, hold that he "gave signal proof of his gentleness and humanity" in receiving back the wife who had deserted him for four years.

Matters were not made easier by the Powell family, who "were in all pretty numerous," quartering themselves on the Miltons. It was for about a year only, as Mary's father died on New Year's Day, 1647, ten weeks before the death of old Mr. Milton, and her mother and the rest of the Powell family stayed not long after. John Milton can have had but little in common with the royalist Powells and, in spite of the house being so filled with his wife's relations and his pupils, he was chiefly conscious of loneliness. Five weeks after his father's death he pours out his heart in a letter to Carlo Dati, a Florentine nobleman, and contrasts the delights of the congenial friendships he had formed in Italy with his present associates: "I am compelled to spend my life in perpetual loneliness." The quiet which was dear to him and essential to his studies was sadly broken by the immoderate noisiness of his guests. As he tells Dati:

> It is often a matter of sorrowful reflection to me that those with whom I have been linked by chance or the law, by propinquity or some connection of no real meaning, are continually at hand to infest my home, to stun me with their noise and wear out my temper, whilst those who are endeared to me by the closest sympathy of tastes and pursuits are almost all denied me either by death or by an insuperable distance of place.

It cannot be expected that Mary Milton should share her husband's intellectual interests, but we may hope that John Phillips correctly reports that they lived "in good accord till her death." In the six years that followed Mary's return she bore him three daughters and a son, before she died in May 1652, "about three days after" the birth of the third daughter Deborah. Deborah and her sisters Anne and Mary survived, but the only son, John, born on 16 March, 1651, died about six weeks after his mother. The tone of Milton's reference to the loss of his first wife and their infant son is discoverable in his belated answer, *Defensio pro Se* (1655), to the abusive *Clamor Sanguinis* which was published in 1652, the year of his bereavement: he says that at that time he "was oppressed with concerns far different" from this controversy. "My health was bad, I was mourning the recent loss of two members of my family, and the light had now quite vanished from my eyes."

Professor W. R. Parker has recently suggested that the lovely and tender sonnet, "Methought I saw my late espoused Saint," commemorates Mary Milton, although from 1725 it has commonly been taken to refer to his second wife.[1] In the sonnet the poet trusts to have "Full sight of her in Heaven without restraint," that is, without the present earthly deprivation of his eyesight. He hopes to see her "once more," which could hardly be used of his second wife, as he was already blind long before he married her.

Jonathan Richardson, in his Life of Milton in 1734, says of the second wife plainly, "We know nothing of her behaviour," but the earliest biographers say that the reconciliation of Milton with his first wife was complete and unmarred by later unhappiness. It was, after all, well that Milton's argument for swift divorce fell on deaf ears, if even the lapse of four years did not kill his affection or make reconciliation impossible. His love for Mary at the first was certainly true with all the ardour of first love, and perhaps it was strong enough to endure. In the sonnet he imagines seeing his wife as a "Saint," which means little more than a departed soul, just as in his "Epitaph on the Marchioness of Winchester" he had envisaged her entering the other world as a "new welcom Saint"; the Puritans were very free with the use of the word Saint. In his dream his dead wife

> Came vested all in white, pure as her mind:
>   Her face was vail'd, yet to my fancied sight,
>   Love, sweetness, goodness, in her person shin'd
> So clear, as in no face with more delight.
>   But O as to embrace me she enclin'd
>   I wak'd, she fled, and day brought back my night.

It would be a happiness to think that Milton's affection for Mary survived all the trials of their long estrangement.

---

[1] The case for the sonnet being a commemoration of Mary Milton is closely argued in W. R. Parker's article, "Milton's Last Sonnet," *Review of English Studies,* July 1945.

Chapter 7

"Areopagitica" (1644) and "Poems" (1645)

It is a relief to turn from the acrimonious and often un-
dignified tracts to the dignity and beauty which distinguish
Areopagitica. John Morley has described this classic defence
of intellectual and spiritual freedom "with its height and
spaciousness, its outbursts of shattering vituperation, its
inflammatory scorn, its boundless power and overflow of
passionate speech in all the keys of passion." It was a protest
against the Order of Lords and Commons made on 14 June,
1643, in more stringent terms than its predecessors. Milton's
plea was at the time ineffectual. The Order continued in force
till the Restoration, when a new Licensing Act was passed on
the basis of the 1637 procedure. This Act was not suffered to
expire till twenty years after Milton's death.

The title-page describes the book as "A Speech of Mr. John
Milton for the Liberty of Unlicenc'd Printing, To the Parliament of England." If Milton cannot address the Commons
from the floor of the House, he does not doubt that his
printed words will carry weight with that assembly. He still
has high hopes of the Long Parliament and of its intention and
ability to introduce an era of greater freedom than England
had yet known. At the outset of his argument he takes it to
be a sign of growing freedom that he can thus publicly, and
with hope of success, urge the Parliament to rescind its own
recent Order.

Milton allows that it is a concern of Church and Commonwealth to keep a vigilant eye upon such publications as may
infect the nation with dangerous mischief, but he warns
against the still greater danger of fettering the expression of
opinion. "We should be wary, therefore, what persecution we
raise against the living labours of public men, how we spill
that seasoned life of man, preserved and stored upon books"
(B., II, 55). If scrupulous care be not taken, there is risk of
plucking up good wheat with the tares, and the world of men

55

would be the poorer for the loss of works which ought to have a life in print:

> As good almost kill a man as kill a good book: who kills a man kills a reasonable creature, God's image; but he who destroys a good book, kills reason itself, kills the image of God, as it were, in the eye. Many a man lives a burden to the earth; but a good book is the precious life-blood of a master-spirit, embalmed and treasured up on purpose to a life beyond life. (B., II, 55.)

Milton is bold to maintain that, unless the will and conscience of a man be defiled, he is immune from harm in learning through books the evil that is in the world. He quotes St. Paul's words, "To the pure, all things are pure"; all kinds of knowledge, whether of good or of evil, may be profitable to man, who had better know of the existence of perverse, erroneous and even vicious opinions, and so be forewarned, than live in a fools' paradise of ignorance. It is this knowledge that tests the judgment of the full-grown man, and distinguishes his mature and deliberate choice of the better from the mere "innocence" of those who in their sheltered lives remain ignorant of "this world of evil, in the midst whereof God hath placed us enavoidably."

> He that can apprehend and consider vice with all her baits and seeming pleasures, and yet abstain, and yet distinguish, and yet prefer that which is truly better, he is the true warfaring Christian. I cannot praise a fugitive and cloistered virtue, unexercised and unbreathed, that never sallies out and sees her adversary, but slinks out of the race, where that immortal garland is to be run for, not without dust and heat. . . . That which purifies us is trial, and trial is by what is contrary. (B., II, 68.)

As Selden had urged, the knowledge of error helps the knowing of truth. Good and evil grow together in this world, and it is the duty and privilege of man to discriminate. The prosecution of truth is in any case difficult, but the difficulty is wantonly increased if knowledge is fettered and learning discouraged. Another paragraph must be quoted, both for its beauty of expression and for Milton's recognition of the slow and difficult task of seeking truth, especially when truth, once discovered, is then suppressed or perverted:

Truth indeed came once into the world with her divine master, and was a perfect shape most glorious to look on: but when he ascended, and his apostles after him were laid asleep, then straight arose a wicked race of deceivers, who, as that story goes of the Egyptian Typhon with his conspirators, how they dealt with the good Osiris, took the virgin Truth, hewed her lovely form into a thousand pieces, and scattered them to the four winds. From that time ever since, the sad friends of Truth, such as durst appear, imitating the careful search that Isis made for the mangled body of Osiris, went up and down gathering up limb by limb still as they could find them. We have not yet found them all, Lords and Commons, nor ever shall do, till her Master's second coming; he shall bring together every joint and member, and shall mould them into an immortal feature of loveliness and perfection. Suffer not these licensing prohibitions to stand at every place of opportunity forbidding and disturbing them that continue seeking, that continue to do our obsequies to the torn body of our martyred saint. (B., II, 89.)

Milton also urges that licensing is bound to fail. It is an ineffective way of stemming vice and error; he compares it to "the exploit of that gallant man, who thought to pound up the crows by shutting his park gate" (70). He regards it as "the greatest discouragement and affront that can be offered to learning and to learned men," if nothing is to be printed which has not passed the censorship of "a prelatical commission of twenty." It was no advantage to have been delivered from the former licensing by bishops and their chaplains, if there was now imposed "a second tyranny over learning." "It is not the unfrocking of a priest, the unmitring of a bishop, and the removing him from off the presbyterian shoulders, that will make us a happy nation" (90).

Milton is well aware that the lapse of the old control of the press by the abolition of the Star Chamber had let loose a spate of controversial books and pamphlets. He reckons, however, that even if some of them may be regarded as heretical or subversive, they are at least a sign of vigorous intellectual life; "for when God shakes a kingdom, with strong and healthful commotions, to a general reforming, it is not untrue that many sectaries and false teachers are then busiest in seducing." But while Parliament and Assembly may be minded to suppress dangerous matter, Milton holds that it is wiser to risk some abuse of freedom than to reimpose an "iron yoke of outward uniformity." He has a sturdy faith in the victory of truth over error: "give her but room, and do not bind her when she sleeps, for then she speaks not true." But if the champions of truth are put on their mettle by the challenge of erroneous opinions, and if they are allowed free utterance, they will cause truth to prevail. "And though all the winds of doctrine were let loose to play upon the earth, so truth be in the field, we do injuriously by licensing and prohibiting to misdoubt her strength. Let her and falsehood grapple; who ever knew truth put to the worse, in a free and open encounter?" (96) Milton knows, as scholars have always known, that freedom is an essential condition of the successful prosecution of truth, and he speaks in the name of them all when he declares: "Give me the liberty to know, to utter, and to argue freely according to conscience, above all liberties" (95).

The principle of intellectual freedom has never been more eloquently stated than in *Areopagitica,* and it still fights for its life in the middle of the twentieth century, in continental Europe at least, if with happily less need among Milton's own countrymen. But if he stated the broad principle with an effectiveness which is still convincing, he characteristically, as in the Divorce treatises, does not grapple with all the practical difficulties and the exceptions which good sense may require. Even his tolerance does not extend to "popery and open superstition," and a few years later he was himself officially concerned with licensing when he served a Government which was nervous of seditious propaganda. Such inconsistencies can be paralleled. One of the earliest and best written defences of religious toleration is Jeremy Taylor's *The Liberty of Prophesying* (1647), but fourteen years later the author found himself set to the uncongenial task of enforcing uniformity in an Irish bishopric and failed practically to maintain the standard he had advocated.

It is a further relief from the contentions of the treatises and from the discord in Milton's own home to note the appearance in the year following *Areopagitica* of "*Poems* of Mr. John Milton, both English and Latin, Compos'd at several times. Printed and publist according to Order." The first collection of his poems is an event of supreme literary importance, though it passed with little notice at the time. The author continued to be known for more than twenty years to come as pamphleteer rather than as poet, except among the discerning few. The author of the anti-episcopal and Divorce treatises had made himself a storm-centre. *Areopagitica* had added to his reputation. Of prose works still to come, *Eikonoklastes* (1649), would be even more controversial than anything he had yet written, and the first and second *Defence of the English People* (1650 and 1654), written in Latin, would make him widely known on the Continent as a political writer, but there were few as yet who had discerned the arrival of a great poet. The production of *Comus* at Ludlow Castle in 1634 would have made him known as poet in select aristocratic circles, and its publication at the instance of Henry Lawes three years later would spread an acquaintance with its exquisite poetry, through the author's name was not given. It is not known that *Lycidas*, which bore his initials only at its first appearance in the little Cambridge commemorative volume of 1638, attracted much attention. Even the appearance of *Poems* in 1645 did not, so far as we know, set the critics talking. In any case the time, the third year of the Civil War, was unfavourable; lovers of the Muses were not too commonly found among the Puritans, and Cavaliers would not be prepossessed in favour of an author who was hitherto known chiefly as a Puritan pamphleteer.

The publisher, Humphrey Moseley, justly prided himself on having an eye for rising poets. As he tells in his preface "To the Reader," he had recently published Edmund Waller's "choice Peeces," and their reception encouraged him to make a similar venture by "bringing into the Light as true a Birth, as the Muses have brought forth since our famous *Spenser* wrote." Moreover, he claims that he has solicited this collection of poems from the author; this may be, as Dr. Tillyard remarks, no more than "the author's conventional Renaissance apology for going into print," but Milton had repeatedly shown his unwillingness to stake his reputation on any works that precede the full maturity of his powers. It was not that he was unaware of the distinction that marked even his early poems—he preserved them, even his *juvenilia,* and would print them sooner or later—but he regarded all that he had hitherto written as the prelude or training-ground for his intended *magnum opus.* The Virgilian motto on the title-page of the 1645 volume prays that his brows may be bound with foxglove, a herb that was believed to avert the evil eye, "lest an evil tongue harm the poet that is to be." It may well be strictly true that the enterprising publisher needed to use his persuasive powers with Milton, and was justified in the pride with which he announced the *Poems:*

> It is not any private respect of gain, Gentle *Reader,* for the slightest Pamphlet is now adayes more vendible than the works of learnedest men; but it is the love I have to our own Language that hath made me diligent to collect, and set forth such *Peeces* both in Prose and Vers as may renew the wonted honour and esteem of our English tongue.

A volume which contained the Nativity ode, the ode "At a Solemn Musick," *Comus, Lycidas, L'Allegro* and *Il Penseroso,* and the sonnets on his passing his twenty-third year and "When the assault was intended to the city," would have eventually established Milton's place among the great English poets, even if he had not lived to write *Paradise Lost* and *Samson Agonistes.* We may be glad that he withheld until the enlarged edition of *Poems* in 1673 the ugly sonnet "On the Detraction which followed upon my writing certain Treatises," either on æsthetic grounds or because he would not in 1645 needlessly affront Puritan opinion at a time when it was desirable to unite it against the royalists. His humour was apt to be heavy-handed. When a lady reported to Dr. Johnson Miss Hannah More's surprise that the author of *Paradise Lost* "should write such poor sonnets," he replied: "Milton, Madam, was a genius that could cut a Colossus from a rock;

but could not carve heads upon cherry-stones." Milton could, in fact, compose exquisitely fine sonnets and short poems, but his violent partisanship was apt to blunt his æsthetic sense, as in the inferior sonnets.

The publisher did Milton a disservice by prefixing to *Poems* a singularly grim and elderly-looking portrait of the author by William Marshall, the engraver who generally worked for Moseley. Milton, who was very conscious of his handsome and youthful appearance, was perhaps unable to persuade the masterful publisher to withdraw the offensive portrait, but he induced Marshall to engrave beneath it four Greek lines, in which the poet invites those who do not know him by face to laugh at "the bad artistic travesty" of the original. It may be presumed that the engraver knew no Greek, and so did not realize that he was engraving his own condemnation.

It should be noted that the volume of 1645 contained no poems written since 1638, except for a few sonnets and some Latin poems. Since his return from Italy Milton's pen had been wholly engaged in writing prose. As the manuscript note-book of his in the library of Trinity College, Cambridge, shows, he was already making lists of possible subjects for his great work, and had not yet decided whether its form should be dramatic or epic. His long preparation and assiduous studies, and his experience of life lived at a great moment in English history, would fit him for treating an heroic subject on the grand scale, but he did not yet embark upon it. At the age of thirty-seven he could hardly think himself no longer ripe for assaying the highest achievement in poetry, but his sense of the gravity of the issues which confronted the nation decided him to devote his abilities to the defence of liberty, as he conceived it. There could be no clearer proof of the nobility of his character than this deliberate postponement of his lifelong design until he should have fulfilled what he thought to have a prior claim upon him. Milton was not only a great poet, but a great Englishman.

Chapter 8

Milton, Defender of Regicide

HITHERTO MILTON's prose writing had not entered the strictly political sphere. He had contended for liberty, the great passion of his life, in the spheres of church reform and the marriage law, and had advocated the freedom of the press and a better system of education. In the *Second Defence of the English People,* published in 1654, he explains why he had selected these topics in preference to the political, and perhaps in retrospect he attributes a more logical and orderly system of proceeding than he had consciously adopted at the time of writing these treatises. It is, for instance, improbable that he would have written just when he did on divorce if the subject had not forced itself upon his notice by his own unhappy experiences. Nor would he have interrupted the series of tracts on divorce by his advocacy of a free press if his own unlicensed tracts had not been brought to the notice of Parliament by the Stationers' Company. It was not unnatural that the order of his polemical treatises should have been occasioned by events that concerned himself, though he always sought to treat the questions, once raised, from a general standpoint without referring explicitly to his personal concerns.

It is otherwise with his first definitely political tract, signed "J.M." He is correct in saying that he did not write on the issue between King and Parliament "till the King, voted an enemy by the Parliament, and vanquished in the field, was summoned before the tribunal which condemned him to lose his head" (B., I, 260). *The Tenure of Kings and Magistrates,* "proving that it is Lawful, and hath been held so throughout all Ages, . . . to call to account a Tyrant, or wicked King, and after due conviction to depose and put him to death," did not affect the decision to execute Charles I, as it was not published till a fortnight after his death. Milton may have begun composing it before the verdict was given, but its purpose was, as he said in 1654, "to reconcile the

63

minds of the people to the event" (B., I, 260), and to discredit the Presbyterians who had shown themselves less disposed to carry the struggle to its logical conclusion than the Independents and the army. Milton had long lost faith in the Presbyterians, and was always ready to belabour them when he had outstripped them in the republican faith which he had come to hold.

The treatise defends regicide in general terms with little direct reference to the case of Charles. He dismisses the "pity" for Charles, pleaded by the less thoroughgoing Puritans, as "no true and Christian commiseration, but either levity and shallowness of mind, or else a carnal admiring of that worldly pomp and greatness, from whence they see him fallen; or rather, lastly, a dissembled and seditious pity, feigned of industry to beget new discord" (B., II, 4).

Milton protests that his writing of this treatise was unsolicited by any of those in authority, and that, after delivering himself of it, he hoped to turn his thoughts to the *History of Britain,* upon which he was already engaged. But, not of his own seeking, he was "surprised by an invitation from the Council of State, who desired my services in the office for foreign affairs" (B., I, 261). Just a month after publishing *The Tenure of Kings* he was sworn in as Secretary of Foreign Tongues to the Council, and he held that office till the Restoration eleven years after. The salary was about £290 a year, which was slightly reduced when his blindness obliged him to have an assistant. His principal duty was to translate into stately Latin the despatches to foreign courts and rulers. As an excellent Latinist he heartily agreed with the decision to employ Latin instead of what his elder nephew calls "the Wheedling Lisping Jargon of the Cringing French," and, as his younger nephew says, Milton had "the manners and genius" of the French "in no admiration." Even so great a mind as Milton's had its limitations and prejudices.

Besides these official and routine tasks, in which Milton must express the mind of the Council rather than his own, he was also encouraged to use his pen in defence of the Commonwealth both at home and abroad. Soon after the king's execution there appeared *Eikon Basilike; the Pourtraicture of His Sacred Majestie in His Solitudes and Sufferings.* No less than forty-seven editions were printed at The Hague and elsewhere in rapid succession. It purported to be the work of Charles himself in captivity, and it inevitably fortified the royalists and confirmed the uneasiness in the minds of many Puritans about the king's execution. Confidence in the new Government was shaken, and it was imperative that the credit of *Eikon Basilike* should be undermined without delay. As John Toland puts it: "This piece, like *Cesar's* last Will, doing more execution upon the Enemy than its Author when alive, *Milton* was commanded to prevent by an Answer those ill effects the *Eikon Basilike* might produce."

The answer, *Eikonoklastes* (breaker of an ikon or image, a term long associated with the Protestant destruction of objects of superstition at the Reformation), appeared on 6 October, 1649. It had nothing like the sale of the book which it attacked. There was a second augmented edition in the next year, and then no further reprint for forty years. Milton's own account, five years after its appearance, is:

A book appeared soon after [the king's execution], which was ascribed to the king, and contained the most invidious charges against the parliament. I was ordered to answer it; and opposed the *Iconoclast* to the *Icon*. I did not insult over fallen majesty, as is pretended; I only preferred Queen Truth to King Charles. (B., I, 261.)

This is finely said, but it is hardly borne out by Milton's treatise. He hints at the author of *Eikonoklastes* not being the king himself, but he finds it more telling in argument to presume the king to be responsible for every statement and the case to be the best that the king could put out for himself. Milton is justified in rebutting every defence which is made in *Eikonoklastes* for the king's folly and untrustworthiness, and this should have been enough. But, with a complete lack of generosity and with real injustice, he dismisses as hypocrisy Charles's genuine piety and his penitence for his desertion of Strafford, and even makes gross insinuations against the purity of his private life. He scoffs at the king's loyalty to "his old Ephesian goddess, called the Church of England" (B., I, 475), and to the Book of Common Prayer, which he describes as "superstitious, offensive, and, indeed, though

Englished, yet still the mass-book" (433). Even if its prayers had been "Manna itself," their continued use, after they had become stale, would "be found, like reserved manna, rather to breed worms and stink" (431). Adherence to "a servile yoke of liturgy" could only be called constancy "if it were constancy in the cuckoo to be always in the same liturgy" (433). And as for the ministers of the Church, "Where was there a more ignorant, profane, and vicious clergy, learned in nothing but the antiquity of their pride, their covetousness, and superstition?" (382). This he says of a Church which included among its ministers since Milton came of age such men as Donne, George Herbert, Robert Sanderson, Hammond, Pearson, Jeremy Taylor, "the ever memorable Mr. John Hales of Eton College," Chillingworth, and Benjamin Whichcote. "All confess," wrote Selden, most critical of men, "there never was a more learned clergy." There were, of course, as well time-servers and careerists, like Montague and Williams, who deserved Milton's lash, but the standard of the Anglican clergy, both for massive learning and for devotion to their spiritual calling, was never higher than in Charles I's reign, and the king numbered among his chaplains some of the most devout and learned. Milton's tirade was not judicial but reckless abuse; so far could partisanship carry him away from a just estimate.

A bigger task than to refute the sophistries and false sentiment of *Eikon Basilike* was soon put upon Milton by the Council of State. Some of the Scots Presbyterians, who were still favourable to the cause of monarchy, had persuaded a notable European scholar, Claude de Saumaise, a professor at Leyden, who Latinized his name as Salmasius, to indict the English people for regicide. His *Defensio Regia* appeared in November 1649, and on the following 8 January the Council, reasonably concerned about the effect which the book might have on the reputation of England abroad, instructed its Latin Secretary to prepare an answer. Shortly before Lady Day, 1651, there was published *Joannis Miltoni Angli Pro Populo Anglicano defensio, contra Salmasii defensionem regiam.* The reputation of Salmasius as a scholar was perhaps above his deserts, but Milton's name was as yet little known on the Continent, though it would become so through his two

Defences in the Latin tongue. In his sonnet "To Mr. Cyriack Skinner upon his Blindness" he could proudly speak of his works in defence of liberty as

> my noble task,
> Of which all Europe talks from side to side.

With his command of the Latin language and his knowledge of English constitutional history he was more than a match for his formidable opponent. His nephew Edward recalls how "our little English David had the Courage to undertake this great French Goliath, to whom he gave such a hit in the Forehead, that he presently staggered, and soon after fell." In fact, the credit of Salmasius at the court of Queen Christina of Sweden fell at once, and he died in 1653 with his *Responsio* to Milton's onslaught finished but not to be published for another seven years, by which time the controversy had lost its interest. On the contrary, six editions, besides a Dutch translation, of Milton's first *Defence* were called for within a twelve-month. Milton held the field and his adversary was routed.

The first *Defence* is tedious, as it seeks to controvert, in the manner of the times, the opponent's statements, one by one, sometimes, as Milton suspects, "replying to some of his fooleries and trifles, as if they were solid arguments." Only now and again he deserts this wearisome *argumentum ad hominem* and rises to an eloquent exposition of some great political principle. It is also in the manner of the times, though not all controversialists descended to that level, to answer personalities with personalities, railing with railing. So Milton addresses his opponent as "thou superlative fool," "you slug you," or calls him "this silly little scholar" and, for his superstitions, "a raving and distracted cuckoo." He does all he can to discredit not only the arguments of Salmasius, but his character also. "My adversary's cause is maintained by nothing but fraud, fallacy, ignorance, and barbarity; whereas mine has light, truth, reason, the practice and the learning of the best ages of the world, of its side" (B., I, 6).

In his preface Milton alludes to bodily indisposition which obliges him "to write by piecemeal, and break off almost every hour." Most serious of all, he was endangering his eyesight by his protracted labours. Even before beginning the first *Defence* he had lost the use of one eye. His nephew Edward says that his uncle's sight "what with his continual Study, his being subject to the Head-ake, and his perpetual tampering with Physick to preserve it, had been decaying for above a dozen years before, and the sight of one for a long time clearly lost." His nephew John says: "Hee was indeed advis'd by his Physitians of the danger, in his condition, attending so great intentness as that work requir'd. But hee . . . to whom the love of Truth and his Country was dearer than all things, would not for any danger decline their defence." Milton himself gives a fuller account in the *Second Defence* of his resolutely facing the danger:

> When I was publicly solicited to write a reply to the Defence of the royal cause, when I had to contend with the pressure of sickness, and with the apprehension of soon losing the sight of my remaining eye, and when my medical attendants clearly announced that, if I did engage in the work, it would be irreparably lost, their premonitions caused no hesitation and inspired no dismay. I would not have listened to the voice even of Æsculapius himself from the shrine of Epidaurus, in preference to the suggestions of the heavenly monitor within my breast; my resolution was unshaken, though the alternative was either the loss of my sight or the desertion of my duty. (B., I, 238).

When he forfeited his eyesight and his opponents cruelly suggested that his blindness was a divine judgment upon him for his defence of a bad cause, he made the most effective and dignified of all his retorts:

> It is not so wretched to be blind, as it is not to be capable of enduring blindness. . . . Let them consider . . . that, in the solace and the strength which have been infused into me from above, I have been enabled to do the will of God; that I may oftener think on what he has bestowed, than on what he has withheld. . . . But, if the choice were necessary, I would, Sir, prefer my blindness to yours; yours is a cloud spread over the mind, which darkens both the light of reason and of conscience; mine

keeps from my view only the coloured surfaces of things, while it leaves me at liberty to contemplate the beauty and stability of virtue and of truth.   (B., I, 236-9.)

He holds that he is more than compensated by the illumination of "an interior light, more precious and more pure." His true friends will show him the greater tenderness and consideration, and he will still be able to "discharge the most honourable duties."

It would have been contrary to human nature if Milton could at all times have maintained this Stoic disregard of his affliction. As we might expect, he alludes to his blindness in varying tones, according to his mood and feeling. The earliest allusion is in the beautiful sonnet, written probably in 1652 when his eyesight failed him completely save for some faint susceptibility to light, at the age of forty-three:

> When I consider how my light is spent
> Ere half my days in this dark world and wide,

his first sad reflection is that it may prevent the realization of his lifelong project of writing a great poem, but God will accept the will for the deed: "They also serve who only stand and wait."

Three years later he proudly tells Skinner what it is that has supported him in the infirmity of his eyes:

> The conscience, Friend, to have lost them over-ply'd
> In Liberty's defence, my noble task.

Long before blindness had overtaken him, the theme of Samson had attracted him, and in his last great poem the blindness of his hero engages his interest for the first hundred lines, though, later, Samson bravely declares that "that which was the worst now least afflicts me"; blindness is a lesser evil than bondage. Yet more movingly, and explicitly of his own person, Milton tells in the famous opening of the third Book of *Paradise Lost* what the deprivation of sight means to him and where he looks for compensation:

> Thus with the Year
> Seasons return, but not to me returns
> Day, or the sweet approach of Ev'n or Morn,

Or sight of vernal bloom, or Summers Rose,
Or flocks, or herds, or human face divine;
But cloud in stead, and ever-during dark
Surrounds me, from the chearful waies of men
Cut off, and for the Book of knowledg fair
Presented with a Universal blanc
Of Natures works to mee expung'd and ras'd,
And wisdome at one entrance quite shut out.
So much the rather thou Celestial light
Shine inward, and the mind through all her powers
Irradiate, there plant eyes, all mist from thence
Purge and disperse, that I may see and tell
Of things invisible to mortal sight.

Milton frankly rejoiced in the discomfiture of Salmasius and enjoyed the European fame which the first *Defence* brought him. But, as his nephew Edward remarks: "Though Salmasius was departed, he left some stings behind; new Enemies started up, Barkers, though no great Biters." One of these anonymous opponents, John Rowland, Milton wisely turned over to John Phillips to deal with. It would have been better for Milton's reputation as a man of judgment if he had similarly ignored the bitter attack upon his character in another anonymous Latin treatise, *Regii Sanguinis Clamor*, "The Royal Blood crying to heaven for vengeance on the English Parricides." Its author was Dr. Peter du Moulin, an Anglican minister, son of a well-known French Protestant divine. The editor, who contributed the preface anonymously, was one Alexander More (Morus), whom Milton described as "part Frenchman, part Scot," "lest one nation should have the too great burden of the entire disgrace of him." Milton took More to be the author of the treatise and, even when More disclaimed it, and the Dutch ambassador supported More's denial, he persisted in attributing the work to him. More was at any rate concerned with the production of *Clamor*, and there is rough justice in Milton's comment, as reported by Aubrey: "Well, that was all one. . . . One of them was as bad as the other." It was more effective for him to represent More as the author, because if *Clamor* traduced Milton, Milton could retaliate by revealing some very discreditable incidents in More's shady career. With a rather ponderous and coarse humour, and with many bad puns, he shows More up as an unprincipled libertine, who had dared to utter "a most scandalous libel" upon Milton's character. While we grudge the many pages devoted to the castigation of "a worthless scribbler," we may yet welcome the *Second Defence* for the light it throws upon Milton's political opinions and upon his own literary ambitions.

The *Second Defence* appeared in May 1654, five months after Cromwell had become Lord Protector. Milton approves his dismissal of the Rump and his assumption of the almost regal Protectorship, though it alienated many of Cromwell's former supporters and associates. "Nothing in the world," says Milton, "is more pleasing to God, more agreeable to reason, more politically just, or more generally useful than that the worthiest man should possess sovereign power. Such, O Cromwell, all acknowledge you to be" (B., I, 288). Once more he defends the English people for "bringing the Tyrant to a scaffold," as a necessary act for the defence of liberty. "It will be sufficient, either for my justification or apology, that I have at least celebrated one of the heroic actions of my countrymen" (299). He believes himself to be defending "the dearest interests, not merely of one people, but of the whole human race, against the enemies of human liberty; as it were in a full concourse of all the nations on the earth" (221). He proudly imagines himself to be addressing, "as I did in my former *Defence,* the whole collective body of peoples, cities, states, and councils of the wise and eminent, through the wide expanse of anxious and listening Europe" (219). Milton, the advocate of liberty, had a far larger audience than the author of *Paradise Lost* was to have, at any rate in his life-time, though after-times would pay more heed to the poet than to the publicist. In some true if incomplete sense he was delivering to the world, in his first and second *Defence of the English People,* that epic "doctrinal and exemplary to a nation," to which he had early dedicated his powers. Never again would he enjoy such full faith in the greatness and moral worth of "God's Englishmen."

The *Second Defence* is even more enduringly valuable for the three long autobiographical passages which it contains.

For more than a score of pages the author discourses upon his character, manner of life, and poetic aims. He always took himself very seriously, and, being fully conscious of his genius, was not withheld by any false modesty from asserting it. No great English poet, not even Wordsworth in *The Prelude,* has given to the public so full an account of himself, and Milton was right in believing that his own generation as well as posterity would be interested in this self-revelation. If a great painter may leave a self-portrait, it is not less allowable or less welcome that an author should do the like; and the more Milton was traduced by his enemies, the more he was disposed to reveal his true character and aims. We owe it to Bishop Hall and his son, to Salmasius and du Moulin and Alexander More, that Milton has told us so much of himself, just as it was Charles Kingsley's attack that gave us Newman's illuminating *Apologia pro Vita sua.*

When at last Milton's controversy with Alexander More ended with the publication of his *Apologia pro Se contra Morum* in August 1655, there was a cessation of his polemical writing until the eve of the Restoration. From 1655 he was relieved from some of the routine duties of the Latin Secretariate "so that, being now quiet from State Adversaries and publick Contests, he had leisure again for his own Studies and private designs." He could resume his *History of Britain* and his compilation of a new *Thesaurus* of the Latin language which was used after his death for a dictionary, published at Cambridge in 1693. The same industrious habit set him at work "framing a Body of Divinity out of the Bible," whether he designed it for his own use in the composition of *Paradise Lost* or whether he originally intended it for publication. It remained unpublished, and was indeed long lost sight of, and first saw the light in 1825 under the title *De Doctrina Christiana.*

It may be presumed that the Latin Secretary was responsible for the manner of expression rather than for the matter which was dictated to him by the Lord Protector and the Council of States, but in one instance at least the matter must have commanded the full assent of the Secretary as well as of general English opinion. This was Cromwell's intervention in favour of the persecuted Vaudois subjects of the Duke of Savoy. The Dukes, who were also Princes of Piedmont, had granted a limited protection within an assigned area to their Protestant subjects, but on 25 January, 1655, the reigning Duke issued an edict ordering the inhabitants of nine communes in the valley of Luserna to move higher up the valley. When they refused to quit their homes, troops were sent to expel them, and the villages were laid waste and many of the inhabitants brutally murdered, while the survivors took to the snow-covered mountains. The news of this cruelty stirred England profoundly.

The Protector, forgetful of the savageries practised by his soldiers five years before at Drogheda and Wexford, came forward as the champion of the Piedmontese. Under his instructions the Latin Secretary on 25 May wrote despatches to the Duke of Savoy, and as well to Louis XIV and his great minister Cardinal Mazarin, since France still adhered to the policy of religious toleration. Letters were also written to the States General of the United Provinces, to the Kings of Sweden and Denmark, and to the city of Geneva. In the letter to the Duke of Savoy it was politic to assume that the barbarities committed in enforcing his edict were done without his knowledge and that he would wish to rescue the survivors from "perishing miserably by cold and hunger." The Protector and his fellow-countrymen confess themselves interested in the Piedmontese sufferers "not by common humanity only, but also by community of religion." Partly as a result of Cromwell's representations and threats and partly because of French interposition the Duke restored the ancient rights by a treaty signed on 18 August. But if diplomatic correspondence with the Duke required a certain polite restraint of language from the Latin Secretary, Milton as poet could vent his strong feeling in the most passionate of all his sonnets, "Avenge, O Lord, thy slaughter'd Saints." Here, more even than in the Latin letters, Milton expressed the English mind, of his own day and of posterity.

Until 1651 Milton had had chambers assigned to him at Whitehall, but in that year he moved to "a pretty garden-house" in Petty France, Westminster, and there he remained till the Restoration. Throughout his London life he generally contrived to have a garden where he could take exercise in safety. When from 1655 he was excused from daily attendance at Whitehall, he was allowed to work at home on the translation of important diplomatic despatches.

A real though short-lived happiness came to him in his second marriage on 12 November, 1656, to Katherine Woodcock. She was twenty-eight years of age, the eldest of four daughters of Captain William Woodcock, an idle and extravagant man who had died about a dozen years before. Woodcock's widow settled at Hackney, then a country suburb, where she had worthy and substantial kinsfolk among her neighbours. The married life of John and Katherine Milton lasted barely fifteen months. A daughter Katherine was born on 19 October, 1657, the mother died of a consumption on the following 3 February, and the child survived her mother only six weeks; mother and daughter were buried in St. Margaret's, Westminster. The nephews have nothing to say of Milton's second wife, unless it was from one of them that Aubrey learnt that she was gently born and of "a peaceful and agreeable humour." Nothing more is known of her, unless Milton's exquisite sonnet to "my late espoused Saint" refers to her, as has been generally believed, and not to his first wife.[1] It is well that this austere man, not easily moved to tenderness, should have been happily mated. His widowed state continued till his third marriage just five years after.

[1] See p. 54.

Chapter 9

Milton's Faith in England

NO ENGLISH WRITER in any age has ever expressed his faith in England with more impassioned ardour and greater eloquence than Milton. It may be well to collect in this chapter, at the expense of a little repetition, some notable expressions of this faith. Inspiring almost all that he wrote was his passionate concern for liberty, and second only to that love was his faith in the English people as having for many generations striven more valiantly to win freedom and valued it more highly than any other modern people. When as a young man in Italy his Italian hosts professed to envy him the Englishman's freedom, he "took it as a pledge of future happiness, that other nations were so persuaded of England's liberty" (B., II, 82).

On his return to England in the summer of 1639 the great struggle for civil and religious freedom was already imminent, and he was soon engaged in controversial writing. His prose treatises have long lost much of their topical interest, and as literature they are disfigured by the scurrilities of the time, but wherever he expresses his faith in England he speaks as a Hebrew prophet would speak of the Chosen Race. To be apostrophized as "God's Englishmen" is an inspiriting call to heroic endeavour, and it has its place in our national literature, but lesser men than Milton have carried the idea to dangerous heights. During the Boer War W. E. Henley stirred his countrymen with patriotic verses acclaiming England as "Chosen daughter of the Lord," and praying that, through successful war,

> The One Race ever might starkly spread,
> And the One Flag eagle it overhead!

But this national egoism does not readily justify itself in the eyes of other peoples, and since Henley's day we have rightly taken offence at the National Socialist myth that the Nordic race was destined to lead the world in culture and was the one race in which God revealed Himself. And when Milton writes, "Let not England forget her precedence of teaching nations how to live," we do well to bear in mind that other nations have often been restive when English statesmen, like Lord Palmerston, took to lecturing them. That we are "God's Englishmen" is a faith better kept for our own inspiration than noised abroad.

In the earliest of his treatises, *Of Reformation in England*, Milton recalls with pride that, with the preaching of Wycliffe, England had "this grace and honour from God to be the first that should set up a standard for the recovery of lost truth, and blow the first evangelic trumpet to the nations, holding up, as from a hill, the new lamp of saving light to all Christendom" (B., II, 368). When he recalled how, as a result of "the precedency which God gave this island," the dawn of "the bright and blissful Reformation" had spread its light to other lands, "methinks a sovereign and reviving joy must needs rush into the bosom of him that reads or hears; and the sweet odour of the returning gospel imbathe his soul with the fragrancy of heaven" (367).

His satisfaction is, however, tempered by the reflection that the Reformation in England went less far than in Scotland and on the Continent. He regrets that Henry VIII "stuck where he did," and that the English reformers, especially "those halting and time-serving prelates," retained so much of the old ceremonies and discipline; but if now "the noisome and diseased tumour of prelacy" could be "cut away from the public body," the English Church would "come from schism to unity with our neighbour reformed sister-churches," which "doubtless with all hearty joy and gratulation will meet and welcome our Christian union with them, as they have been all this while grieved at our strangeness and little better than separation from them" (B., II, 407). He scouts the attempts to enforce episcopacy and liturgy on the Scots, "to ingage the unattainted Honour of English Knighthood, to unfurl the streaming Red Cross . . . for so unworthy a purpose as to force upon their fellow-subjects that which themselves are weary of, the skeleton of a mass-book" (406). He bids the two nations, English and Scots, "never to be disunited" but to make common cause "to settle the pure worship of God in his church, and justice in the state" (407).

Events would soon prove, even to Milton himself, that the bulk of the English people were not willing to exchange their own church system, with all its defects, for the Scottish presbytery. It would not be long before Milton's passing preference for presbyterianism would be abandoned when he saw the intolerance and the rigid discipline of the Westminster Assembly divines. He was on stronger ground when he asked his readers not to forget "what numbers of faithful and freeborn Englishmen" had gone overseas to find the religious freedom which was denied them at home. The treatise ends with an eloquent prayer that God who did "build up this Britannic empire to a glorious and enviable height, with all her daughter-islands about her," and had scattered the Spanish armada, may now "stay us in this felicity" and deliver England from tyranny at home:

> Then, amidst the hymns and halleluiahs of saints, some one may perhaps be heard offering at high strains in new and lofty measures to sing and celebrate thy divine mercies and marvellous judgments in this land throughout all ages; whereby this great and warlike nation . . . may press on hard to that high and happy emulation to be found the soberest, wisest, and most Christian people at that day, when thou, the eternal and shortly-expected King, shalt open the clouds to judge the several kingdoms of the world, and distributing national honours and rewards to religious and just commonwealths, shalt put an end to all earthly tyrannies, proclaiming thy universal and mild monarchy through heaven and earth. (B., II, 418.)

In his third treatise, *Animadversions* (1641), Milton asserts even more emphatically that God, though "being equally near to his whole creation of mankind," "hath yet ever had this island under the special indulgent eye of his providence" (B., III, 70). "Who is there," Milton asks, "that cannot trace thee now in thy beamy walk through the midst of thy sanctuary, amidst those golden candlesticks, which have long suffered a dimness amongst us through the violence of those that had seized them, and were more taken with the mention of their gold than of their starry light? . . . Every one can say, that now certainly thou hast visited this land" (71). If the writer "now for haste snatches up a plain ungarnished present," as a thankoffering in prose for "so many late deliverances," the time will come when God has "settled peace in the church and righteous judgement in the kingdom," and then the poet will "perhaps take up a harp, and sing thee an elaborate Song to Generations" (72). His immortal work shall be a poem telling of England's greatness under the good hand of God's special providence.

By the time that he published *The Reason of Church Government* in February 1642, the prospects of a more thorough Reformation were greatly advanced. The Commons had passed the Grand Remonstrance and impeached the bishops and ended their "Egyptian tyranny." The king had failed to arrest the five members and had left the capital. Now was the opportunity. The natives of some other countries "may haply be better composed to a natural civility and right judgement" than the Englishman, "but if he get the benefit once of a wise and well-rectified nurture, which must first come in general from the godly vigilance of the church, I suppose that wherever mention is made of countries, manners, or men, the English people, among the first that shall be praised, may deserve to be accounted a right pious, right honest, and right hardy nation" (B., II, 470). Then he allows himself a long digression to tell of his hope that he may "leave something so written to after-times, as they should not willingly let it die" (478). Poetic abilities he accounts to be "the inspired gift of God," and they

are of power, beside the office of a pulpit, to inbreed and cherish in a great people the seeds of virtue and public civility, to allay the perturbations of the mind, and set the affections in right tune; to celebrate in glorious and lofty hymns the throne and equipage of God's almightiness, and what he works, and what he suffers to be wrought with high providence in his church; to sing the victorious agonies of martyrs and saints, the deeds and triumphs of just and pious nations, doing valiantly through faith against the enemies of Christ (479).

It is, then, for "a great nation" that he means to celebrate its achievements, and to this high end he will dedicate all his powers when he shall be free to leave the urgent calls of the present.

Milton's unbounded faith in England reaches its acme and its most eloquent expression in *Areopagitica* (1644). In pleading for a removal of the licensing restrictions he bids the lords and commons of England "consider what Nation it is whereof ye are, and whereof ye are the governors: a Nation not slow and dull, but of a quick, ingenious, and piercing spirit; acute to invent, suttle and sinewy to discourse, not beneath the reach of any point the highest that human capacity can soar to. . . . Yet that which is above all this, the favour and the love of Heaven we have great argument to think in a peculiar manner propitious and propending towards us. Why else was this Nation chosen before any other, that out of her, as out of *Sion,* should be proclaimed and sounded forth the first tidings and trumpet of Reformation to all *Europe?*" (B., II, 90). Then, with even more assurance than in any previous treatise, Milton proclaims the speedy coming of a new Reformation:

> Now once again by all concurrence of signs, and by the general instinct of holy and devout men, as they daily and solemnly express their thoughts, God is decreeing to begin some new and great period in his Church, even to the reforming of Reformation itself; what does he then but reveal himself to his servants, and as his manner is, first to his Englishmen? (91.)

Milton describes the contemporary London as "a City of refuge, the mansion house of liberty," where not only are the munitions of war being forged, but where "there be pens and heads there, sitting by their studious lamps, musing, searching, revolving new notions and ideas wherewith to present, as with their homage and their fealty, the approaching Reformation" (91). He professes himself not troubled by the variety of opinion: "there must be many schisms and many dissections made in the quarry and in the timber, ere the house of God can be built." If there was any uneasiness in his mind at all this theological turmoil, he overcomes his apprehensions in a sentence which, though the best known of any prose that he wrote, can hardly here be omitted:

> Methinks I see in my mind a noble and puissant Nation rousing herself like a strong man after sleep, and shaking her invincible locks: methinks I see her as an Eagle mewing her mighty youth, and kindling her undazzled eyes at the full midday beam; purging and unscaling her long-abused sight at the fountain itself of heavenly radiance; while the whole noise of timorous and flocking birds, with those also that love the twilight, flutter about, amazed at what she means, and in their envious gabble would prognosticate a year of sects and schisms. (94.)

Chapter 10

Disillusion

MILTON'S FAITH in the English people would never again be so unreservedly expressed as in 1644. He became increasingly disillusioned in turn with the Presbyterians, the Long Parliament, the people at large, and even to some extent with Cromwell.

His disappointment with the Westminster Assembly divines began almost at once when they gave a hostile reception to his divorce treatises and advocated a strict licensing of the press. In the second sonnet, "On the Detraction which followed upon my writing certain Treatises," he angrily complains:

> But this is got by casting Pearl to Hoggs;
> That bawle for freedom in their senceless mood,
>   And still revolt when truth would set them free.
>   Licence they mean when they cry libertie;
> For who loves that, must first be wise and good.

And he is as emphatic in *Areopagitica:*

> If some who but of late were little better than silenced from preaching shall come now to silence us from reading except what they please, it cannot be guessed what is intended by some but a second tyranny over learning: and will soon put it out of controversy, that Bishops and Presbyters are the same to us, both name and thing. (B, II, 83.)

His disillusion with the Long Parliament, while the Presbyterian majority controlled it before Colonel Pride effected its "purge" on 6 December, 1648, is exhibited in the remarkable digression which he placed at the head of the third Book of his *History of Britain*, four Books of which he had finished before he became Latin Secretary in March 1649. When he came to publish the *History* in 1670 this digression was omitted, almost certainly because, as Sir Charles Firth maintains,[1] he was unwilling to condemn the failures of those with whom he had once worked, now that they were out of office. It was, however, posthumously printed in 1681 as *Mr. John Milton's Character of the Long Parliament and Assembly of Divines.* By 1649 he had come to believe that the great opportunity of reforming England and its religion had been missed and had led to a "ridiculous frustration." Liberty had been put "like a bridle into the hands" of the Parliament and Assembly, but they had failed to use it. "When once the superficial zeal and popular fumes that acted their new magistracy were cooled, and spent in them, strait every one betook himself, setting the commonwealth behind, his private ends before, to do as his own profit or ambition led him" (B., V, 236). Faction and favour carried the day, justice was first delayed and then denied, and though there were some "men of wisdom and integrity" in the Parliament, "the greatest part" proved unworthy of the confidence placed in them.

"And if the state were in this plight, religion was not in much better." Those who had declaimed with greatest fervour against the abuses in the prelatical church and were loudest in acclaiming "their boasted reformation" were not ashamed to become themselves non-resident ministers and pluralists, and, in spite of their many protests against compulsion in religion, they distrusted "the virtue of their own spiritual weapons" and looked to the secular arm to enforce their "spiritual tyranny." "There hath not been a more ignominious and mortal wound to faith, to piety, . . . nor more cause of blaspheming given to the enemies of God and truth, since the first preaching of reformation" (239). He sums up his indictment in words which contrast sadly with what he had said in the earlier treatises:

> For Britain (to speak a truth not often spoken), as it is a land fruitful enough of men stout and courageous in war, so is it naturally not overfertile of men able to govern justly and prudently in peace, trusting only in their mother-wit. . . . Valiant indeed and prosperous to win a field, but to know the end and reason of winning, unjudicious

[1] Firth, *Essays, Historical and Literary,* 1938, pp. 98-100.

and unwise: in good or bad success alike unteachable. (B., V, 240.)

A further shock to Milton's faith in the English people was afforded by their reaction to the beheading of Charles I. He could not disguise from himself that it provoked, besides the inevitable horror of the royalist half of the nation, an uneasiness of mind or even positive distress in a considerable part of the other half. It argued some real courage in Milton to come forward as the principal literary defender of this unpopular act. In *The Tenure of Kings* he notes that many "begin to swerve and almost shiver at the majesty and grandeur of some noble deed, as if they were newly entered into a great sin" (B., II, 5). Ministers of the Gospel who had lately spoken of hewing Agag in pieces and destroying the Amalekites hip and thigh were quickly become "apostate scarecrows" and begin to talk of "the Lord's anointed" and of the duty owed to "a lawful magistrate." Fortunately, he says, there were others "indued with fortitude and Heroick virtue to fear nothing but the curse written against those that do the work of the Lord negligently," and who will "for the deliverance of their country" make an end of their worst enemy.

In *Eikonoklastes* he recognized that, except for "some few who yet retain in them the old English fortitude and love of freedom," the rest showed "a besotted and degenerate baseness of spirit" (B., I, 313). He was fain to ascribe this "debasement of mind in the people" to the "pulpit-stuff" of hypocritical preachers and to factious politicians, but these explanations could not for long satisfy him. The markedly aristocratic tone of his mind made him increasingly distrustful of the many. His faith was rather in the wise and virtuous few who, in the interest of the many, would assume present control until better education had trained the many to be worthy of a share in government; "there are but few, and those men of great wisdom and courage, that are either desirous of liberty or capable of using it." "Liberty hath a sharp and double edge, fit only to be handled by just and virtuous men." The purpose of government, he holds, is "that good men may enjoy the freedom which they merit, and the bad the curb which they need" (B., V, 240). Hence in the *Second Defence* (1654) he applauded Cromwell for his decision to dispense for a while with parliaments and for having "alone remained to conduct a government, and to save the country."

In 1654 Milton believed that Cromwell was singularly fitted to bear rule because he had achieved self-mastery, for there is no virtue which he admires more than the subordination of passion to reason. The Protector is "the favoured object of the divine regard," "elevated by the special direction of the Deity to the highest pinnacle of power" (B., I, 290). Yet with all Milton's lofty praise there are mingled some misgivings and a note of warning against unqualified dictatorship, Cromwell would do well to share "the protection of our liberties" with some others of tried virtue and capacity, like Fleetwood and Lambert, Algernon Sydney and Henry Lawrence, who have distinguished themselves in the senate or in the field. He is especially warned to "leave the church to its own government" and to deprive it of the power of persecution, which would remain so long as he persisted in his project of an established church with State-paid ministers. He must "no longer suffer two powers, so different as the civil and the ecclesiastical, to commit whoredom together, and by their mutual and delusive aids in appearance to strengthen, but in reality to weaken, and finally to subvert, each other" (B., I, 293). On the separation of Church and State Milton is irreconcilably opposed to Cromwell's policy; in the very last year of the Protectorate he would deliver himself even more vehemently in *The likeliest Means to remove Hirelings from the Church*.

Milton also warns the Protector against an excessive multiplication of laws, since "Liberty is the best school of virtue" (B., I, 294). Better education will do more to furnish virtuous citizens than prohibitive laws. Above all, let there be "free discussion of truth without any hazard to the author"; to fetter the minds of men is the worst of all tyrannies.

Milton's latest theories of government are announced on the eve of the Restoration, briefly in *A Letter to a Friend concerning the Ruptures of the Commonwealth* and in his *Letter to General Monk* on "The present means and brief delineation of a free Commonwealth," and more fully in *The Ready and Easy Way to establish a free Commonwealth*. The months between Oliver Cromwell's death and the recall of Charles II, with all the intermediate uncertainty that hung over General Monk's intentions, afforded a golden opportunity for the designers of constitutions. James Harrington's *Oceana* (1656), recommending a constitution on the Venetian model, was much discussed, especially in the Rota Club over which Milton's friend, Cyriack Skinner, sometimes presided. Milton surrendered less completely than Harrington to the Venetian myth of its age-long perfect balance, the best modern counterpart of the classical republics, but some of its features he borrows for his scheme. It was natural that a scholar like Milton should always have had some tenderness for the republics of ancient Greece and Rome, although as late as 1641 he had not dismissed the idea of a constitutional monarchy. He believed in the value of a "mixed" constitution, containing the three classical elements, monarchy, aristocracy (in the Greek sense of the rule of "the best" rather than of the well-born), and democracy; any one of the three adopted absolutely was liable to its special abuse, but a balance of the three would avoid the abuses. In his treatise *Of Reformation* (1641) he had written:

> The best-founded commonwealths and least barbarous have aimed at a certain mixture and temperament, partaking the several virtues of each other state. . . . There is no civil government that hath been known, no not the Spartan, nor the Roman, . . . more divinely and harmoniously tuned, more equally balanced as it were by the hand and scale of justice than is the commonwealth of England; where under a free and untutored monarch, the noblest, worthiest, and most prudent men, with full approbation and suffrage of the people, have in their power the supreme and final determination of highest affairs. (B, II, 408.)

The monarchical element in Milton's scheme of 1660 would not be a single magistrate, for now he could not brook "the fond conceit of something like a Duke of Venice," severely limited though the powers of the Doge were. He had once accepted Cromwell's one-man rule, when many Parliamentarians took offence at it, but now he would make it a condition of holding office that single rule should be abjured. The monarchical element would be represented in a Council of State, elected by, and responsible to, the Grand Council, a name borrowed from Venice. He thought that the "Norman or French" word *Parliament* had "outlived its honour by soe many dissolutions" and was become "a monument of our Ancient Servitude." From henceforth Parliament "would be better called the Grand or General Council of the Nation" (B., II, 107). A striking feature of his Grand Council, which was also found at Venice, was that it was to be perpetual, only the vacancies caused by death or "just conviction of some crime" needing to be filled by fresh elections. His experience of a Long Parliament which had had a much-interrupted life of twenty years might have given him pause, but he did not think that his countrymen could "be advantaged by successive and transitory parliaments," which were "much likelier continually to unsettle rather than to settle a free government, to breed commotions, changes, novelties, and uncertainties, while all minds are in suspense with expectation of a new assembly, and the assembly, for a good space, taken up with the new settling of itself" (B., II, 122). It must be presumed that he had not overlooked Aristotle's criticism of the Spartan government: "When the legislator enacted that the members of this Council should hold their office for life, he did not consider that the understanding grows old as well as the body," and that old men are slow to make the changes which time may make desirable.

The part of the people in Milton's programme of government was nominally impressive but in fact subordinate. He attributed the fall of ancient Rome to the "popularities" having secured too much power and upset the balance. He was well aware that a really free election of a new Parliament by the entire body of the English electors would bring back the monarchy. He would, therefore, restrict the franchise to those well affected to the republic. He held that there was "in number little virtue, but by weight and measure wisdom working all things" (B., II, 112). It was more just "that a less number compel a greater to retain their liberty, than that a greater number, for the pleasure of their baseness, compel a less most injuriously to be their fellow-slaves" (133). In this restricted franchise "the better part" would stand for the whole people and more securely safeguard the liberty of all. He would yet further ensure the election of fit men to the Grand Council by an elaborate procedure of successive winnowings,

> not committing all to the noise and shouting of a rude multitude, but permitting only those of them who are rightly qualified, to nominate as many as they will; and out of that number others of a better breeding, to choose a less number more judiciously, till after a third or fourth sifting and refining of exactest choice, they only be left chosen who are the due number, and seem by most voices the worthiest (B., II, 126).

Milton added one remarkable provision for the development of popular government in a narrower field where its exercise could be safely allowed. He recommended that every county should be made "a kind of subordinate commonalty or commonwealth," with similar provision for the chief cities. He anticipated that this local government would be exercised chiefly by "the nobility and chief gentry," and that it would save the localities from over-much interference by the Grand Council. "They shall have none then to blame but themselves" if the administration be not good. They would have the right to declare their views by deputies whom they might send to the Grand Council, on the understanding that "this their judgement declared shall submit to the greater number of other counties or commonalties" (135). The procedure bears some resemblance to the Soviet system in modern Russia.

When in the spring of 1660 writs were being sent out for the election of a Convention Parliament, Milton declared with what seems an unwarranted optimism: "Now is the opportunity, now the very season, wherein we may obtain a free commonwealth, and establish it for ever in the land, without difficulty or much delay" (121). It is difficult to suppose that he felt as hopefully as he wrote, or that he expected General Monk to take notice of the recommendations he had made in the letter which accompanied *The Ready and Easy Way*. Milton was mainly concerned, less with constitution-making, than with a last desperate effort to avert the restoration of the monarchy. He dreaded the evident possibility that, after the long successful "contestation with tyranny," the English people would so little know how to use their liberty as "basely and besottedly to run their necks again into the yoke which they have broken" (119). He foresaw that, if the Stuart monarchy was restored, England would "soon repent" when she saw "the old encroachments coming on by little and little upon our consciences," and would be "forced perhaps to fight over again all that we have fought" and tread "back again with lost labour all our happy steps in the progress of reformation" (115). Some part of his prophecy would be fulfilled within his own lifetime. As early as 1667 Pepys, who had described the delirious joy of the people at the Restoration, is writing in his Diary:

> It is strange how everybody do now-a-days reflect upon Oliver, and commend him, what brave things he did, and made all the neighbour princes fear him; while here a prince, come in with all the love and prayers and good liking of his people, who have given greater signs of loyalty and willingness to serve him with their estates than ever was done by any people, hath lost all so soon, that it is a miracle what way a man could devise to lose so much in so little time.

By the time that a second edition of *The Ready and Easy Way* was called for in April 1660, Milton realized that "the good old cause" was doomed and that his treatise might prove to be no more than "the last words of our expiring liberty," yet he will boldly publish it, come what may:

> But I trust I shall have spoken persuasion to abundance of sensible and ingenuous men; to some, perhaps, whom God may raise from these stones to become children of reviving liberty; and may reclaim, though they seem now choosing them a captain back for Egypt, to bethink themselves a little, and consider whither they are rushing; to exhort this torrent also of the people, not to be so impetuous, but to keep their due channel; and at length recovering and uniting their better resolutions, now that

they see already how open and unbounded the insolence and rage is of our common enemies, to stay these ruinous proceedings; justly and timely fearing to what a precipice of destruction the deluge of this epidemic madness would hurry us, through the general defection of a misguided and abused multitude. (B., II, 138.)

Milton's altered feeling about the value of popular judgment is still more strongly expressed a few years later in the scornful words which he assigns to Christ in *Paradise Regained* when the tempter holds out to Him the way to win "the people's praise":

And what the people but a herd confus'd,
A miscellaneous rabble, who extol
Things vulgar, & well weigh'd, scarce worth the praise,
They praise and they admire they know not what;
And know not whom, but as one leads the other;
And what delight to be by such extoll'd,
To live upon thir tongues and be thir talk,
Of whom to be disprais'd were no small praise?
His lot who dares be singularly good.
Th' intelligent among them and the wise
Are few, and glory scarce of few is rais'd.

(P.R., III, 49.)[2]

Already on the eve of the Restoration Milton was knowingly running grave risks. Besides his maximum offence of having been the foremost literary defender of regicide and the unsparing detractor of King Charles the Martyr, he was, when the Restoration was clearly in view, asserting his unshaken faith in republicanism and his contempt for Charles II and his courtiers. Apart from those who had signed the death-warrant of Charles I, there could be few persons more likely to incur the utmost penalty than the author of *The Tenure of Kings* and *Eikonoklastes*, who had also served as Latin Secretary throughout the Commonwealth period.

Monk had wisely recommended Charles II to promise, before he returned to England, a general indemnity in generous terms, and this policy was adopted in the Declaration

[2] P.R. is used for excerpts from *Paradise Regained*.

of Breda, which was announced to the Convention Parliament on the memorable First of May when the Restoration was voted. The king promised a free pardon "to all his subjects who should within the next forty days profess their loyalty," "excepting only such persons as shall hereafter be excepted by Parliament." It was, therefore, for Parliament to name those who were to be excepted in the Bill of General Pardon, Indemnity and Oblivion, which had its first reading on 9 May. After some days' discussion it was unanimously agreed that none should be put to death but seven of the regicides, and on 6 June the seven were named. Three days later it was carried by a small majority that "twenty and no more" of those other than regicides who had seriously compromised themselves should be excepted from pardon but receive no other punishment than to be perpetually incapacitated from holding offices of state. Milton's name did not appear in the list of twenty named in the Act, which received the royal assent on 29 August.

Edward Phillips, writing in 1694, states that "till the Act of Oblivion came forth," his uncle remained in hiding in "a Friend's House in Bartholomew-Close," and that Andrew Marvell, member for Hull, acted vigorously in his behalf and made a considerable party for him." It is true that on 16 June the House ordered the burning by the common hangman of the first *Defence of the People of England* and *Eikonoklastes*, and the arrest and prosecution of the author; but it may be because, as Dr. Johnson suggests, he was "not perhaps very diligently pursued," that he escaped arrest at the time, and the Act of Oblivion of 29 August presumably cancelled the order. According to John Phillips, Milton "early sued out his Pardon; and by means of that, when the Serjeant of the House of Commons had officiously seised him, was quickly set at liberty." The Journal of the House records an Order "that Mr. Milton, now in custody of the serjeant-at-arms attending this House, be forthwith released, paying his fees." His friends successfully pleaded that the serjeant's fees were excessive, and they were reduced. Milton had no more to fear as he was not "excepted" in the Act, and therefore could not be further prosecuted in respect of anything he had written before the Restoration. John Phillips says that his uncle "demeaned himself peaceably" and was even offered State employment, though the latter statement is unsupported by other evidence and is improbable.

Milton's fortunes were considerably reduced. He had lost his office as Latin Secretary and many of his investments, and he had to surrender a small property which he had bought out of the estates of Westminster Abbey, which were now recovered. He had, however, his father's patrimony and other means, which enabled him to live with comfort and decency. He had always lived frugally and temperately. It was not in any material loss that he suffered, so much as in the frustration of his high hopes for Church and State. He had celebrated in prose what he believed to be a national achievement, but the England which had now abandoned "the good old cause" could no longer be the subject of an epic. It may not be altogether a loss that he should have substituted for a national theme the universal one of the destiny of mankind.

In the only surviving letter of Milton which is dated after the Restoration he writes to Peter Heimbach, Counsellor to the Elector of Brandenburg, who had heard a rumour that the poet had died of the Great Plague in 1665:

> The virtue you call statesmanship (but which I would rather have you call loyalty to my country), after captivating me with her fair-sounding name, has, so to speak, almost left me without a country. . . . One's country is wherever it is well with one. (B., III, 522.)

Chapter 11

"Paradise Lost"

As MILTON announces at the beginning of Book IX of *Paradise Lost*, "this Subject for Heroic Song Pleas'd me long choosing, and beginning late." He believed it to be a "higher Argument" than those chosen by Homer, Virgil, Tasso and Spenser, and better fitted to his genius and experience than the Arthuriad which he had once contemplated. He has, indeed, some misgivings—that the northern climate is unfriendly to the Muses, or that he writes in "an age too late" when the degenerate world will not welcome heroic verse, or that his own years will "damp" his spirit, unless his "Celestial Patroness" vouchsafes to inspire him.

The theme of the Fall of Man had been in his mind for nearly twenty years before he settled down to work upon it. Edward Phillips states that "Satan's exclamation to the Sun" (P.L., IV, 32-41) was composed "about 15 or 16 years before ever his Poem was thought of, which verses were intended for the Beginning of a Tragoedie which he had designed, but [he] was diverted from it by other businesse." These lines, he says, "were shewn to me and some others, as designed for the very beginning of the said Tragedy." According to the same witness, a serious start was made upon *Paradise Lost*, no longer in dramatic but epical form, "about 2 yeares before the K. came-in, and finished about 3 yeares after the K's Restauracon." It may have taken a little longer than Phillips states, but it appears to have been finished by the late summer of 1665, when Milton lent the manuscript to his young Quaker friend, Thomas Elwood, to take home and read at leisure. Whether Milton held it back for further revision another year and a half is not known, but the contract with the publisher, Samuel Simmons, "next door to the Golden Lion in Aldersgate," was not made till 27 April, 1667, and copies of the first edition in small quarto were on sale by the end of the following August at the price of three shillings. By the agreement Milton was to receive £5 at once, and £5 for each of the first three editions after the sale of 1,300 copies of each. Actually he received two sums of £5, and his widow in 1680 commuted any further claims on Simmons for £8. Lord Camden finely remarks that Milton "knew that the real price of his work was immortality, and that posterity would pay it."

We may sometimes have wondered how the blind poet composed so long a poem without the use of pen and paper. It has been the habit of some poets, like Wordsworth, to compose in their heads on a solitary walk and to commit the lines to paper on their return. Dr. Johnson composed Latin poems in bed to occupy his mind on sleepless nights. We can, however, learn something more precise about Milton's methods of composition from his nephews. One curious fact is stated by Edward Phillips—"His Vein never happily flow'd but from the Autumnal Equinoctial to the Vernal, and that whatever he attempted"—at other seasons—"was never to his satisfaction, though he courted his fancy never so much; so that in all the years he was about this Poem, he may be said to have spent but half his time therein." Mrs. Milton corroborates this statement when she says that "her husband used to compose his poetry chiefly in the winter." This is the opposite of what we should have expected as, in the Latin elegy on the Approach of Spring, written at the age of twenty, he writes: "Do I deceive myself, or is strength coming back into my songs also, and have I, thanks to the bounty of spring, inspiration at my call? The spring, the spring that gave me inspiration, shall be the theme of songs it inspires."

There is also circumstantial evidence of Milton's composing in bed. John Phillips tells how the poet "waking early (as is the use of temperate men) had commonly a good Stock of Verses ready against his Amanuensis came; which if it happend to be later than ordinary, hee would complain, Saying *hee wanted to bee milkd.*" The poet himself alludes to what he hoped to obtain

> Of my Celestial Patroness, who deignes
> Her nightly visitation unimplor'd,
> And dictates to me slumbring, or inspires
> Easie my unpremeditated Verse.

(P.L., IX, 21.)

Jonathan Richardson, writing in 1734, enlarges upon this habit of Milton's:

> He frequently Compos'd lying in Bed in a Morning ('twas Winter Sure Then). I have been Well inform'd, that when he could not Sleep, but lay Awake whole Nights, he Try'd; not One Verse could he make; at Other times flow'd *Easy his Unpremeditated Verse*, with a certain *Impetus* and *Æstro* [œstro, poetic inspiration], as Himself seem'd to Believe. Then, at what Hour soever, he rung for his Daughter to Secure what Came.

Aubrey says that Deborah, the youngest daughter, was her father's amanuensis, but she was only twelve or thirteen when *Paradise Lost* was finished, and it would have been rather heartless to fetch her out of bed in the early hours of a winter's morning, even if at that age she was equal to taking down the poet's lines with their many learned allusions and difficult words. Her usefulness to the poet, which need not be questioned, probably belongs to the years when he was composing *Paradise Regained* and *Samson Agonistes*. Milton was obliged to excuse his eldest daughter Anne from such service "by reason of her bodily Infirmity and difficult utterance of Speech"; she "grew more and more decrepit" and signed her name to her father's will with a cross only. He was dependent on members of his household for first aid in taking down what he had composed in bed; at later hours of the day he had many willing helpers, including former pupils, to write and read for him. Their imperfect efforts would be corrected on the arrival of Edward Phillips, who describes himself as his uncle's "chief Amanuensis"; "I had the perusal of it [*Paradise Lost*] from the very beginning; for some years, as I went from time to time, to Visit him, in a Parcel of Ten, Twenty, or Thirty Verses at a Time, which being Written by whatever hand came next, might possibly want Correction as to the Orthography and Pointing."

The last words are important, as no poet, not even Robert Bridges, has been more insistent than Milton on the forms of spelling and the punctuation which he desired. It must have been a laborious task for Edward Phillips to spell out to the blind poet all doubtful words and indicate orally what stops and spelling he was using. For instance, Milton sought to distinguish by spelling between the emphatic and unemphatic uses of the personal pronoun; thus, in the *Errata* for the first edition of *Paradise Lost* there is the instruction, "for *we* read *wee*" (II, 414). He was particular about spelling, especially when it might affect sound or scansion, e.g. *sovran, faln, stolne, perfet, thir, ammiral, facil.* Jonathan Richardson, with a painter's eye, has preserved what he has heard "concerning the Posture he was Usually in when he Dictated, that he Sat leaning Backward Obliquely in an Easy Chair, with his Leg flung over the Elbow of it."

A national epic was no longer possible for Milton, who was already disillusioned even before the close of the Protectorate by the failure of the "new reformation" from which he had expected so much, by the mere exchange of one ecclesiastical tyranny for another, by the Protector's adherence to the policy of a paid ministry, and by the fickleness of "the multitude." He could not, therefore, celebrate in triumphant song a regenerated England, and instead he must spend his powers upon a more universal theme. His case is not unlike that of Wordsworth, his warmest admirer and truest successor among the English poets. Wordsworth had hailed the French Revolution as the dawn of a new day for all mankind, but after a while he saw its ideals deserted for a common war of conquest. In despair of man's political activities he took comfort in contemplating the native dignity and worth of individual man, his "unconquerable mind" and his brave endurance of ills "for the glory that redounds Therefrom to human kind." He resolved that he would

> through the human heart explore my way,
> And look and listen, gathering whence I may
> Triumph, and thoughts no bondage can restrain.

So, Milton, baffled in his hopes for collective man, retains his faith in the power of individual man, an Adam or a Samson, to achieve self-mastery and interior peace.

Milton assays a cosmic theme and treats it on a far greater scale than Wordsworth ever achieved. Within the narrow framework of the old story of Adam's Fall he will fashion his reflections upon man's freedom to choose between good and evil and the eternal issues which depend on the victory of reason over passion. Freedom is, as always, Milton's unremitting concern, but his experiences, both personal and political, have taught him that the only freedom worth having is in obedience to the voice of reason, and that freedom is forfeited by disobedience. So the arch-angel admonishes Adam towards the close of the poem:

> yet know withall,
> Since thy original lapse, true Libertie
> Is lost, which alwayes with right Reason dwells
> Twinn'd, and from her hath no dividual being:
> Reason in man obscur'd, or not obeyd,
> Immediately inordinate desires
> And upstart Passions catch the Government
> From Reason, and to servitude reduce
> Man till then free.
>
> (XII, 82.)

And as it is with individuals, so is it with nations:

> Yet somtimes Nations will decline so low
> From vertue, which is reason, that no wrong,
> But Justice, and some fatal curse annext
> Deprives them of thir outward libertie,
> Thir inward lost.
>
> (XII, 97.)

This is the counterpart of the warning words which Milton addressed to the English people in *The Ready and Easy Way*.

The theme of man's testing and destiny is high enough to engage all his powers, and he makes sublime poetry of it. There are, however, two main difficulties in the way of the great epic finding appreciative readers. The first is the vast scope of the poem. It ranges over all time and space, and even beyond them both. It depicts heaven and earth and chaos, the imagined utterances of superhuman beings, events before the emergence of man upon earth, the history of man from his creation and, by prophecy, to the end of time, and his eternal destiny. And all this portentously wide survey hinges upon the single act of Eve's disobedience and Adam's misguided concurrence:

>   her rash hand in evil hour
> Forth reaching to the Fruit, she pluck'd, she eat:
> Earth felt the wound, and Nature from her seat
> Sighing through all her Works gave signs of woe,
> That all was lost.
>
> (IX, 780.)

Not all the mountain of theological speculation in the Christian centuries built upon a single chapter of *Genesis* is comparable with Milton's structure, heaven-high and hell-deep. Where the Bible is explicit, he appears to accept it literally, even if also he sees it to have far-reaching symbolical significance. As he puts in the mouth of Raphael (V, 571):

>   what surmounts the reach
> Of human sense, I shall delineate so,
> By lik'ning spiritual to corporal forms,
> As may express them best, though what if Earth
> Be but the shaddow of Heav'n, and things therein
> Each to other like, more than on earth is thought?

Where the Bible is silent, his imagination is unfettered and has full rein. No difficulties deter him and no sense of awe withholds him. There are no mysteries for Milton, no reticence before the Ineffable.

A contrast is inevitably made with the other supremely great writer of a Christian epic. In the Beatific Vision which is the climax of *The Divine Comedy* there is the rose of glorified saints and there are the nine choirs of angels, but there is no Divine voice, and it is light only that indicates the Divine presence: "a light there is in heaven which maketh the Creator visible unto the creature, who, only in beholding Him, hath its own peace." Milton sometimes, though too rarely, chooses the better way, and his noble diction is admirably fitted for such purpose, as, for instance, when he describes the "sacred Song" of the host of angels round the throne:

> Thee Father first they sung Omnipotent,
> Immutable, Immortal, Infinite,
> Eternal King; thee Author of all being,
> Fountain of Light, thy self invisible
> Amidst the glorious brightness where thou sit'st

> Thron'd inaccessible, but when thou shad'st
> The full blaze of thy beams, and through a cloud
> Drawn round about thee like a radiant Shrine,
> Dark with excessive bright thy skirts appeer,
> Yet dazle Heav'n, that brightest Seraphim
> Approach not, but with both wings veil thir eyes.
>
> (III, 372.)

It is far otherwise when Milton makes the Almighty argue like a lawyer. Pope has pronounced once for all the common judgment of men on these unhappy efforts:

> Milton's strong pinion now not Heav'n can bound,
> Now serpent-like, in prose he sweeps the ground,
> In Quibbles Angel and Archangel join,
> And God the Father turns a School-Divine.

In other respects Milton is not less successful than Dante in treating sublime themes with dignity and reverence. There remains, however, the difficulty of giving naturalness to the conduct and language of super-human beings, whether celestial or infernal, and even Adam and Eve in their unfallen state are far removed from human experience. Milton overcame this difficulty at any rate better than any lesser man or inferior poet could have hoped to do.

The second main obstacle to the full appreciation of *Paradise Lost* by the reader to-day is the obsolete and unattractive nature of much of Milton's theology. This is not, indeed, a fatal obstacle. The Æneid does not suffer seriously from our not accepting Virgil's traditional mythology. It is a little more difficult when Milton presents his own strongly Puritan and individual interpretation of a Christian tradition which still maintains a hold upon many of his readers. The main lines of that tradition are presented in *Paradise Lost*—the frustration of the Divine intention for man by his surrender to sin and his consequent need of a Redeemer—but the emphasis is not the characteristically Christian one. Milton, with his pride and self-sufficiency, is almost a Pelagian in his belief that man can work out his own salvation if he will but subordinate his passions to the dictates of reason. He does not deny the need of "supernal Grace contending With sinfulness of Men"

(XI, 359), but it is less prominent than the insistence on self-control. Nor is this deficiency made good in *Paradise Regained*.

A more serious defect is his delineation of the Almighty, who shares much of the hardness of Milton himself. God's outraged anger and threats of punishment are more conspicuous than His mercy and forgivingness. He shows no sadness or pity for the fallen angels who once had their place in their Creator's service, and the plight of fallen man appeals more to the Son than to the Father. It is not the Father who calls out man's love, though He may awe him by His omnipotence. It would not content Milton that we should admire the sublimity of his poetry, because this limitation would defeat his purpose, which was, quite certainly, not only to please as poet but to teach as prophet. At the outset of the poem he announces his purpose to "justifie the wayes of God to men," and, however he may have succeeded with earlier generations, he no longer is able to convince. Yet it would be unfair to him not to recognize the strength and sincerity of his religious conviction, and he can hardly be blamed for expecting that later ages would continue to think as he did.

The first two Books reveal Milton at his greatest. The scene opens with the rebel angels prostrate and dumbfounded at their downfall into "utter darkness." Satan, undaunted, rallies them with words breathing courage and defiance:

> What though the field be lost?
> All is not lost; the unconquerable Will,
> And study of revenge, immortal hate,
> And courage never to submit or yield:
> And what is else not to be overcome?
> That Glory never shall his wrath or might
> Extort from me.
>
> (I, 105.)

Then follows the rapid building of his palace or Pandemonium, and in it the fallen angels gather for the Great Consult, over which he presides "high on a Throne of Royal State." Shall it be war or peace? Reminiscences of debates in the Long Parliament, doubtless, helped the poet to contrast the counsels of the different speakers. Moloch recklessly gives his sentence for open war; even if they do but shake the Almighty's throne and fail of victory, they will taste the sweets of revenge. A very different counsellor is Belial, "in act more graceful and humane." Do we well to challenge the Omnipotent, who may respond by annihilating us, and can there be anything worse than the cessation of "this intellectual being"? If instead we accept our defeat, "Our Supream Foe in time may much remit His anger" and even ignore us if we avoid His attention; and, as we become used to hell, we shall feel its pains less, and its darkness will lighten. Belial seems likely to carry a majority with him, as he has the art to "make the worse appear the better reason." Mammon fortifies the view that there is no hope of unthroning "Heav'ns Lord"; let them, indeed, refuse conciliation if it is offered, because it would mean "Forc't Halleluiahs," which would be intolerable to proud spirits. If we "live to ourselves" and rely on our own skill and resourcefulness, here in hell are the materials for building a "nether Empire" of great wealth and magnificence.

Such applause followed Mammon's speech that his counsel would have prevailed, had not Beelzebub intervened; his very aspect commanded attention:

A Pillar of State; deep on his Front engraven
Deliberation sat and publick care;
And Princely counsel in his face yet shon,
Majestick though in ruin.

(II, 302.)

He bids them dismiss the facile notion that the King of Heaven will fail to extend His rule over hell itself, which is not the safe retreat that they fondly imagine, but their dungeon. Instead of "hatching vain Empires," let them keep to what is practicable. They cannot hope to conquer the Almighty, but they can harm the apple of His eye. He takes up a hint that Satan has already dropped, that they should turn their attention to God's new creation, man, in the new World that He has made for him. They can either exterminate the "punie habitants" of Earth and win it for themselves, or seduce them so that God would in vengeance hurl "his darling Sons" to perdition; "this would surpass Common revenge," and "spite the great Creatour." But, to carry out this project will require a scouting of infinite hazard to locate this new World, and there is general reluctance to "undertake the perilous attempt." This is Satan's opportunity, and he wins universal esteem and "awful reverence" when he announces his resolve to go and to share the honour with none. The decision is accepted, and Milton takes occasion to contrast the unanimity of devils with the warring discords of men:

> O shame to men! Devil with Devil damn'd
> Firm concord holds, men onely disagree
> Of Creatures rational, though under hope
> Of heavenly Grace; and God proclaiming peace,
> Yet live in hatred, enmitie, and strife
> Among themselves, and levie cruel warres,
> Wasting the Earth, each other to destroy:
> As if (which might induce us to accord)
> Man had not hellish foes anow besides,
> That day and night for his destruction waite.
>
> (II, 496.)

The opening Books of *Paradise Lost* are such a triumphant success that many readers find their interest never again so greatly stirred in the Books that follow. And this fact has the added difficulty that Milton has so successfully presented Satan, the indomitable rebel against tyranny, that many, like Shelley, have been tempted to find him the hero of the epic. We can detect some of the reasons for Milton's success. He wrote these Books while he still hoped against hope that the Commonwealth would endure and lead on to a better polity than England had known before. Again, Milton was himself a rebel at heart, and there is not a little of his own temper in his Satan, who is universally allowed to be the greatest creation in the poem. He may have even realized as he went further in the poem that he had been too succesful in portraying Satan's heroic greatness and needed to reduce his stature. It is incredible that he meant Satan to be the hero. He knew well enough in his heart, though he would not confess it to men, that pride was his own keenest temptation, and that he must learn the humility which was the Christian grace most difficult for him to acquire.

He takes pains, therefore, to show that Satan's pride, which we have begun by admiring, was in the end his undoing and that it led him to absurdity. It is not enough that Satan "through pride" should resent God's proclamation of His Son as vice-gerent and make it the ground of rebellion, but he must make the preposterous claim that he and his fellow-angels were "self-begot, self-rais'd by thir own quick'ning power." He who had once proudly boasted

> The mind is its own place, and in it self
> Can make a Heav'n of Hell, a Hell of Heav'n

is soon driven to confess, "Which way I flie is Hell; my self am Hell." Before long he reveals himself as the Father of Lies, mean and lustful. The dignity that he showed when presiding in Pandemonium is quite gone when the messengers of the Almighty find him in the Garden of Eden "Squat like a Toad, close at the eare of Eve," and we see him later as a serpent upon his belly. When he returns to hell and meets the fallen angels in full assembly, and reports boastfully of his success in seducing Man, he does not receive the acclamation he expected:

> So having said, a while he stood, expecting
> Thir universal shout and high applause
> To fill his eare, when contrary he hears
> On all sides, from innumerable tongues
> A dismal universal hiss, the sound
> Of public scorn . . .
>   he would have spoke,
> But hiss for hiss returned with forked tongue
> To forked tongue, for now were all transform'd
> Alike, to Serpents all as accessories
> To his bold Riot.
>   (X, 504.)

There is nothing left in Satan to admire except his skill and his reckless defiance.

If *Paradise Lost*, the "Heroic Song," must have a hero, is it then the Son of God? In His face

> Divine compassion visibly appeerd,
> Love without end, and without measure Grace,
>   (III, 141.)

At the heavenly conference in Book III, which is the counterpart of the Great Consult in hell in the previous Book, the
Father, perceiving Satan on his evil errand to seduce mankind,
foretells his success and the doom of Adam and "his whole
posteritie," unless some one is willing to "pay the rigid satisfaction, death for death." Just as the appeal to the fallen
angels for one who shall volunteer for a hazardous undertak-
ing met with silence in hell, until Satan offered himself, so
when the Father asks for a redeemer of "Man's mortal crime,"
wondering if there "dwels in all Heaven charitie so deare,"
there is silence, broken after a pause by the Son exclaiming:

> Behold mee then, mee for him, life for life
> I offer, on mee let thine anger fall;
> Account mee man; I for his sake will leave
> Thy bosom, and this glorie next to thee
> Freely put off, and for him lastly die
> Well pleas'd, on me let Death wreck all his rage.
>
> (III, 236.)

After judgment has been pronounced on Adam and Eve for
their transgression, the Son as "Priest" and "Advocate and
propitiation" presents their penitent prayers. And Michael
foreshows how hereafter the Redeemer by being "nail'd to the
Cross" will pay the penalty which mankind could not pay.
Milton duly states the traditional Christian faith, but the part
played by the Redeemer in this survey of the whole of human
history is not made prominent enough for Him to be regarded
as the hero of the epic.

There remains Adam. He possesses many admirable qualities—intelligence, dignity, courtesy, piety, affection—but he is
hardly heroic except for his resolve to share Eve's fate. His
fall is not due to sensuality, but to a weak surrender to uxo-
riousness. There is a certain momentary levity in his becoming
his wife's accomplice

> Against his better knowledge, not deceav'd,
> But fondly overcome with Female charm.
>
> (IX, 998.)

Adam is no primitive man, but a highly developed intellectual.

Milton's description of him is not unlike what his younger contemporary, Dr. South, intended when he maintained that 'an Aristotle was but the rubbish of an Adam, and Athens but the rudiments of Paradise."

Eve also has no likeness to primitive woman. She has "a virgin majestie," a queenly bearing and she rightly calls out Adam's devotion. Her fall is due to what are commonly regarded as feminine failings; she yields to the tempter's flattery of her beauty, to the vanity that attracts her to the notion that she may "be seen a Goddess among Gods," and to mere curiosity; it was only in a minor degree that she yields to sensual desire, though, once she has bitten into the apple, "Greedily she ingorg'd without restraint, And knew not eating Death." It is also woman-like that she cannot brook the thought that, if she alone should die, Adam may be "wedded to another Eve"; better, she thinks, that he should share her sin and her fate. In her submissiveness to her husband Eve fulfilled all that Milton required of a wife, save only when in self-will she roamed the Garden without his protection and so fell a prey to the tempter. Afterwards she blames him for not forbidding her to go into danger. She had failed to abide by her earlier mind which she had before expressed to Adam:

> God is thy Law, thou mine: to know no more
> Is womans happiest knowledge and her praise.
> With thee conversing I forget all time,
> All seasons and thir change, all please alike.
>
> (IV, 637.)

After the Fall she ultimately returns to that attitude of mind and declares

> both have sin'd, but thou
> Against God onely, I against God and thee.
>
> (X, 930.)

We cannot to-day accept Milton's masculine view—"He for God only, she for God in him"—but we may be glad that, after the first mutual recriminations and Adam's ugly explosion against womankind (X, 888-908), Adam is content that they should no further "blame each other" but strive

In offices of Love, how we may light'n
Each others burden in our share of woe.

(X, 960.)

And though they must leave the earthly Paradise, the ang
bids Adam know he need not regret it if by virtues an
"Charitie the soul of all the rest" he shall come to possess "
Paradise within thee, happier farr" (XII, 587). "The Worl
was all before them," and with "Providence thir guide" ou
first parents "hand in hand" set forth hopefully on "thir sol
tarie way."

Addison was surely right when he said that "he that look
for an hero" in *Paradise Lost* "searches for that which Milto
never intended." Instead we may admire the heroic greatnes
of the poem and the presentation of its vast theme with mas
terly skill and in language that has never been surpassed fo
dignity and musical rhythm. When we recall Aubrey's repor
that Milton "pronounced the letter R very hard," we ca
imagine the extraordinary effectiveness of his reciting sucl
lines as those which describe the opening of Hell Gates:

on a sudden op'n flie
With impetuous recoile and jarring sound
The' infernal dores, and on thir hinges grate
Harsh Thunder, that the lowest bottom shook
Of *Erebus*.

(II, 879.)

Milton had carried through to a successful conclusion thi
poem in which he daringly sought the "Empyreal Aire," i
spite of blindness, defamation and danger. He speaks in hi
own person at the opening of Book VII:

though fall'n on evil dayes,
On evil dayes though fall'n, and evil tongues;
In darkness, and with dangers compast round,
And solitude; yet not alone, while thou
Visit'st my slumbers Nightly, or when Morn
Purples the East.

(VII, 25.)

There are dull and even prosy stretches in the long poem, such as Michael's rather perfunctory statement of the Christian faith, the theological arguments and the discussion of angels' digestion. But the grand manner is almost always maintained and everything bears the unmistakable stamp of Milton's style. Nowhere is there any carelessness, and seldom such an oversight as when he makes Adam say, "how glad would lay me down As in my Mothers lap," though he is described as "not of woman born." The early biographer, Jonathan Richardson, was enthusiastic, but he had warrant for saying:

> A Reader of *Milton* must be Always upon Duty; he is Surrounded with Sense, it rises in every Line, every Word is to the Purpose; There are no Lazy Intervals, All has been Consider'd, and Demands and Merits Observation. Even in the Best Writers you Somtimes find Words and Sentences which hang on so Loosely you may Blow 'em off; *Milton's* are all Substance and Weight; Fewer would not have Serv'd the Turn, and More would have been Superfluous.

Chapter 12

"Paradise Regained" and "Samson Agonistes"

PARADISE REGAINED is not so much a sequel to *Paradise Lost* as a companion-picture. In the earlier poem Satan has tempted our first parents and they lose Paradise; in the later, Satan's more subtle temptations ignominiously fail to move "the perfect Man," and the "Angelic Quires" proclaim His victory:

> now thou hast aveng'd
> Supplanted *Adam,* and by vanquishing
> Temptation, hast regain'd lost Paradise.
>
> (IV, 607.)

But this is not the Gospel evaluation of events; it was not by His superiority to the temptation in the wilderness that the Christ of the Gospels restored fallen man, but by His sacrificial death. In *Paradise Lost* Michael has set forth in orthodox terms the doctrine of the Atonement, but the Cross is not the subject of the later poem.

The closing words of *Paradise Regained* show that the successful emergence from the Temptation qualifies the "Queller of Satan" to enter upon His "glorious work," which is "to save mankind." But Milton does not himself attempt this high theme. There may be many good reasons why he shied at taking this central doctrine of the Christian faith. The very full treatment of the Passion and Crucifixion in the four Gospels would have allowed him little freedom for the use of his great imaginative powers. Failure here would be more serious than failure to handle the story from *Genesis* effectively. It may also be remembered that he appended a note to his early poem, *The Passion:* "This Subject the Author finding to be above the yeers he had, when he wrote it, and nothing satisfi'd with what was begun, left it unfinisht." There are, besides, many indications that, though the doctrine of the Cross is duly mentioned in both poems, it was not central

in his thinking and did not command his full assent. Milton's
Christ—dignified but lacking in tenderness, quick to show
"disdain" and contemning the multitude "of whom to be dis
praised were no small praise," acquainted with pagan history
and thought—is more like John Milton than the carpenter of
Nazareth.

Satan also has changed since *Paradise Lost*. He is no longer
the heroic rebel, leading the forlorn host, but a smooth
scheming spirit, urbane and ready with compliments to his
opponent's character and ideals, until all his wiles have
failed, and then he attempts to terrorize Him with a sudden
storm. He is shrewd enough to realize that coarser temptations
will have no success. He brushes aside Belial's suggestion,
"Set women in his eye and in his walk," and argues:

> Therefore with manlier objects we must try
> His constancy, with such as have more shew
> Of worth, of honour, glory, and popular praise;
> Rocks whereon greatest men have oftest wreck'd.
>
> (II, 225.)

In one instance only does Satan wholly misconceive his adversary. Towards the close of His long fast the Son of God
dreams of how the ravens brought Elijah "bread and flesh"
and how he "drank of the brook." Then Satan confronts
Him with "A Table richly spred, in regal mode" (II, 340),
with fish and game, pastry and wines, while Ganymedes and
Naiads are in attendance, and there are flowers and music.
"I am afraid," wrote Charles Lamb, "the poet wants his
usual decorum in this place. . . . This was a temptation fitter
for a Heliogabalus. The whole banquet is too civic and culi-
nary, and the accompaniments altogether a profanation of
that deep, abstracted, holy scene. The mighty artillery of
sauces, which the cook-fiend conjures up, is out of propor-
tion to the simple wants and plain hunger of the guest." But
perhaps Milton only wanted to show up Satan's stupidity in
thus overshooting the mark.

On other occasions the tempter shrewdly takes for granted
that the Son of God is wholly set on the work of Redemption
and can only be tempted if wealth and power and learning
are shown to be means for accomplishing that work. The offer

of wealth is easily spurned, for Christ and Mammon have nothing in common; nor is He to be lured to seek dominion by force of arms:

> what do these Worthies,
> But rob and spoil, burn, slaughter, and enslave
> Peaceable Nations, neighbouring, or remote,
> Made Captive, yet deserving freedom more
> Than those thir Conquerours, who leave behind
> Nothing but ruin wheresoe're they rove,
> And all the flourishing works of peace destroy?
>
> (III, 74.)

But Satan knows how to appeal to Christ's compassion: will not the acquisition of power enable Him to relieve the poor?

The second temptation seems the likeliest to succeed. Will not the Redeemer best learn the self-control and the trained reason, which are so needful for one who means great achievement, by studying the philosophy and literature of the ancient world? Milton knows well how to present, though it be in Satan's mouth, the glories of Greece, Plato's Academe, and "the Stoic severe"; and Christ also had previously praised "poor Socrates," ranking him next after "patient Job" (III, 95-9). But now "our Saviour" makes His longest reply, in which He says that "he who receives Light from above, from the fountain of light," needs no other doctrine from Greek or Roman sage. All that they have to give

> Will far be found unworthy to compare
> With *Sion's* songs, to all true tasts excelling.
>
> (IV, 346.)

Twenty years before, Milton had averred that the Biblical songs "not in their divine argument alone, but in the very critical art of composition, may be easily made appear over all the kinds of lyric poesy to be incomparable" (B., II, 479). Still, it is surprising that the humanist, who had so dearly loved and imitated the classical writers and was even yet to follow Greek models in *Samson Agonistes,* could bring himself to put into Christ's mouth this uncompromising repudiation of ancient culture and wisdom as being "Thin sown with aught of profit or delight." One is driven to suspect that Milton, as age creeps upon him and his earthly hopes are shattered, is thrown back upon his ultimate spiritual resources but it must mean considerable tension between the surviving humanist that he still is and the Puritan that he is still more

There is also a corresponding austerity in the composition of *Paradise Regained*, which has far less of ornament and imagery than its predecessor. There are, indeed, some passages of the old beauty, as when the morning after the fury of the storm is described:

> Thus pass'd the night so foul till morning fair
> Came forth with Pilgrim steps in amice gray;
> Who with her radiant finger still'd the roar
> Of thunder, chas'd the clouds, and laid the winds.

(IV, 426.)

And the descriptions of ancient Rome and Athens, of the banquet and the storm, give legitimate opportunities for the old magnificence. In a single line the poet can bring the Orient before our eyes when he writes, "Dusk faces with white silken Turbants wreath'd" (IV, 76). And if there is less ornament in *Paradise Regained*, the accustomed Miltonic grandeur is seldom wanting. Though the general reader has commonly failed to appreciate the austere poetry of this poem to the full, the poets, like Coleridge and Wordsworth, have highly praised and loved it. Milton himself, as his nephew Edward relates, "could not bear with patience any such thing when related to him" as that the later poem was "much inferior" to the earlier.

In view of the stern repudiation of Greek literature which Milton attributes to Christ in *Paradise Regained*, it is not a little singular that the same volume contains *Samson Agonistes*, which is nearer to Greek tragedy than any other great work in the English language. Although the theme is from the Hebrew Bible, its treatment owes much to Greek models, as its author describes it in his preface. The introduction of the Chorus especially, he says, is "after the Greek manner, and still in use among the Italians." And there are other features resembling Greek tragedy: the few characters, the important rôle of the messenger, the duologues with a line or two apiece for each interlocutor, the irony which allows the hearer to see a point in words which convey no such meaning to the speaker, and the unexpected reversal of circumstance. But if the form and style are Greek, the spirit is Hebraic and reflects Milton's Puritan mind.

Into no poem of his did Milton put more of himself, and he can deliver himself freely under cover of the story of Samson. Like Samson, he had taken impulsively a wife from among the Philistines, he was afflicted with blindness, he had championed the deliverance of his people who in the end would rather have "bondage with ease than strenuous liberty" (l. 271), and now in age he was impotent, impoverished, neglected. Can he help questioning sometimes whether God, whose ways are "past finding out," has deserted His champion and suffered His cause to fail? If he can but express his sufferings and his misgivings, it will give him relief and bring him at the close of the poem to "calm of mind, all passion spent."

The action of *Samson Agonistes,* again like many Greek tragedies, belongs to a single day, the feastday of the Philistine god Dagon. He who on other days was "Eyeless in Gaza at the Mill with slaves" (l. 41) is this day freed from servile toil and led by a guiding hand to a bank where he can enjoy the sun's rays and "the breath of Heav'n fresh-blowing, pure and sweet." Here he can find

> Ease to the body some, none to the mind
> From restless thoughts, that like a deadly swarm
> Of Hornets arm'd, no sooner found alone,
> But rush upon me thronging, and present
> Times past, what once I was, and what am now.
>
> (l. 18.)

Bitterly he blames himself for his present plight: "Sole Author I, sole cause" of all that has befallen him—captivity, blindness and impotence; it was because he had been "swoll'n with pride" and "proudly secure" that he had weakly fallen into the snare of a woman's "fair fallacious looks" (l. 533). The Chorus and his aged father Manoah in vain seek to comfort him, but he has nothing now to wish for but death, "the welcom end of all my pains" (l. 576).

A worse trial awaits him when the Chorus announces the

approach of Dalila "like a stately Ship, . . . With all her bravery on, and tackle trim" (l. 714). He scouts her "feign'd remorse"; he will not suffer himself to be again "entangl'd with a poysnous bosom snake" (l. 763), and he cries at her "Out, out, Hyœna." When, after much vain colloquy and specious explanations, she asks that she may come closer and touch his hand, he exclaims

> Not for thy life, lest fierce remembrance wake
> My sudden rage to tear thee joint by joint.
> At distance I forgive thee, go with that.
>
> (l. 952.)

The eloquent Harapha of Gath, who next visits Samson, is summarily and rudely dismissed, much as Milton had dealt with Salmasius, the European scholar. The Chorus warns him that "His Giantship," who has gone away "crestfall'n," may make mischief with the Philistine lords; yet they cannot but applaud the spirit which has roused Samson from his depression to show again the old heroic temper:

> Oh how comely it is and how reviving
> To the Spirits of just men long opprest!
> When God into the hands of thir deliverer
> Puts invincible might
> To quell the mighty of the Earth, th' oppressour,
> The brute and boist'rous force of violent men
> Hardy and industrious to support
> Tyrannic power, but raging to pursue
> The righteous and all such as honour Truth;
> He all thir Ammunition
> And feats of War defeats
> With plain Heroic magnitude of mind
> And celestial vigour arm'd.
>
> (l. 1268.)

Sure enough, trouble soon develops; Samson is summoned to come and make sport before the lords. At first he refuses, but, before the officer returns with a second summons, he feels "some rouzing motions" which decide him to go, expecting some unknown achievement which will make the day memorable "by some great act." Little do they suspect it, but the Philistines are bringing upon them their destroyer; here is irony at its finest point. Samson goes, and is not seen again, but soon a messenger arrives with the news that, with a last straining effort, Samson has shaken the "two massie Pillars" which support the temple roof and has involved in one common burial the "choice nobility and flower" of his enemies and their destroyer himself. Whether this final act of undiscriminating revenge deserves it or not, the poet gives Manoah a quatrain of the finest lines in all English literature to pronounce upon his dead son:

> Nothing is here for tears, nothing to wail
> Or knock the breast, no weakness, no contempt,
> Dispraise, or blame, nothing but well and fair,
> And what may quiet us in a death so noble.
>
> (l. 1721.)

After being a widower for just five years Milton married for the third time Elizabeth Minshull, thirty years younger than himself. They settled at Artillery Row, Bunhill Fields, which was to be Milton's home for the rest of his life, except for the year of the Great Plague, when the young Quaker, Thomas Elwood, found him "a pretty box" in the Buckinghamshire village of Chalfont St. Giles. According to the evidence of his brother Christopher, when Milton's nuncupative or word-of-mouth will was disputed by his daughters, the poet "complained, but without passion, that his children had been unkind to him, but that his wife had been very kind and careful of him." The daughters appear to have found it irksome to attend on their blind father and to read to him in languages which they did not understand. They also resented his third marriage, and, some four or five years before he died, they had left home to learn a trade.

Milton's nephew Edward gives a similar account, which has told heavily against the poet as a rather formidable and exacting parent. It is well, however, to balance against these accounts the fact that his youngest daughter Deborah in her old age spoke with warm affection and admiration of her father, and added that "he was delightful company, the life of the conversation," and had "an unaffected chearfulness and civility." This testimony is confirmed by other witnesses.

So far from being soured and morose, as Dr. Johnson imagined, Milton was "affable in Conversation, of an equal and chearful Temper"; "he play'd much upon an Organ he kept in the House," and he "would be cheerful even in his gowt fitts and sing." He enjoyed the solace of tobacco and an abstemious use of wine. Jonathan Richardson preserves an account which he had derived from one of the poet's contemporaries:

> I have heard many Years Since that he Us'd to Sit in a Grey Coarse Cloath Coat at the Door of his House, near *Bun-hill* Fields Without *Moor-gate,* in Warm Sunny Weather to Enjoy the Fresh Air, and So, as well as in his Room, received the Visits of People of Distinguish'd Parts, as well as Quality. and very Lately I had the Good Fortune to have Another Picture of him from an Ancient Clergy-man in *Dorsetshire,* Dr. *Wright;* He found him in a Small House, he thinks but One Room on a Floor; in That, up One pair of Stairs, which was hung with a Rusty Green, he found *John Milton,* Sitting in an Elbow Chair, Black Cloaths, and Neat enough, Pale, but not Cadaverous, his Hands and Fingers Gouty, and with Chalk Stones. among Other Discourse He exprest Himself to This Purpose; that, was he Free from the Pain This gave him, his Blindness would be Tolerable.

Dryden, Marvell and other men of letters had the highest regard for Milton's poetry, and "foreigners of note" sought him out.

The end came very peacefully on 8 November, 1674, "with so little pain or Emotion, that the time of his expiring was not perceiv'd by those in the room." He was buried beside his father in the parish church of St. Giles Cripplegate at "the upper end of the chancell at the right hand." His widow survived him fifty-three years, dying in her native Cheshire in 1727 in her ninetieth year. In the same year his last surviving daughter, Deborah Clarke, died at the age of seventy-five, leaving a daughter Elizabeth, married to one Thomas Foster, a Spittlesfield weaver. It is pleasant to remember that in 1749 Samuel Johnson, who was an unsympathetic biographer of

Milton, though a hearty admirer of *Paradise Lost*, promoted a subscription in relief of Elizabeth Foster, by this time infirm and in straitened circumstances. He persuaded his friend David Garrick to give a benefit performance of *Comus* in Drury Lane Theatre on 5 April, 1750, and himself wrote a Prologue for Garrick to recite. Johnson could rightly claim that it was required by "the honour of letters, the dignity of sacred poetry, the spirit of the *English* nation, and the glory of human nature" that this token of gratitude should be paid to "the granddaughter of the author of *Paradise Lost*," "our incomparable Milton."

Chapter 13

Milton's Doctrine of God

THE THREE great poems of Milton's later years have all of them religious themes, and a full understanding of them necessitates some consideration of his religious ideas. No such scrutiny is required for an understanding of his earlier religious poems or of his treatises written before 1645, as up to that date at least he professed the received opinions of the orthodox Puritan of his day.

Little light can be afforded on Milton's personal beliefs from the tenets of any particular church, as his strong individualism always withheld him from giving unqualified allegiance to any church. Bred in the Church of England, he had not in his twenty-fifth year wholly dismissed the intention of taking orders in that church. His criticism of the English Church was less on matters of doctrine than on its discipline. He objected especially to the episcopal discipline, which he called "prelacy," and for a short while he placed his hopes in a presbyterian remodelling of the church, as many of those episcopally ordained were at this time planning. John Toland says of Milton's successive loose attachments:

> In his early days he was a Favorer of those Protestants then opprobriously cal'd by the name of *Puritans:* In his middle years he was best pleas'd with the *Independents* and *Anabaptists,* as allowing of more Liberty than others, and coming nearest in his opinion to the primitive practice: but in the latter part of his Life, he was not a profest Member of any particular Sect among Christians, he frequented none of their Assemblies, nor made use of their peculiar Rites in his Family.

It may be added that, though never formally attached to the Quakers, he had considerable sympathy with their trust in "the inner light." In his latest treatise, *Of True Religion,* published a year before his death, he even speaks of the Church of England as "our church" (B., II, 516), but it need not imply personal allegiance any more than his being married in church or being buried in his parish church. His infrequent church-going may be explained by his blindness and other infirmities, but is more probably due to his finding greater satisfaction in his private meditations and unremitting study of the Bible. He had no conscious need of personal attachment to any church and its ordinances.

In his earlier writings, both verse and prose, Milton's expressions are orthodox and even dogmatically expressed. Thus he ends his treatise, *Of Reformation,* with an eloquent prayer in which, after addressing each of the Persons of the Trinity, he apostrophizes "one Tripersonal Godhead," using a term which he may even have invented, as no earlier use of it has been found. In the later stages of his theological development he would be impatient of all such "scholastic notions," as he terms them. He might tolerate them as matters of opinion without regarding them as "necessary to salvation." By the time he came to compose *Paradise Lost* he had travelled far from the orthodoxy of earlier years and was conscious that on some doctrines he differed from "the received opinions." This development in his religious ideas affects our understanding of the poem. And here comes in the important and much-disputed question as to how far the posthumous treatise, *De Doctrina Christiana,* can be used to interpret *Paradise Lost.* There is not room in this short book to discuss fully this debatable point, but the nature of the debate can be indicated.

Already in the early 'forties, when Milton was teaching his nephews, we learn from Edward Phillips that one of their Sunday occupations was to write "from his own dictation some part, from time to time, of a Tractate which he thought fit to collect from the ablest of Divines, who had written of that Subject; *Amesius, Wollebius,* &c. viz. A perfect System of Divinity." William Ames, an English Puritan, who had become a professor at Franeker in the Netherlands, was the author of a well-known digest, *Medulla Theologiae,* which was translated into English in 1642 as *The Marrow of Sacred Divinity.* Johan Wolleb published at Amsterdam in 1633 a *Compendium* of theology which ran into many editions, there and at Oxford. Though Milton began with a compilation based on these two Calvinistic books, he was not in the end content to be a mere compiler, and, though he continued to use their framework as a guide, he set about, on being relieved from daily attendance as Secretary in 1655, "the framing of a Body of Divinity out of the Bible." The original purpose of such a disquisition was that it "might be useful in establishing my faith or assisting my memory," "a precious aid for my faith," and doubtless also as a foundation for his great religious poems.

The work engaged him more or less for the rest of his life. When he came to write the preface, probably at the end of the work, as is the way of authors, he certainly contemplated publication. With his usual assurance the preface is headed "John Milton, to all the Churches of Christ, and to all who profess the Christian faith throughout the world." As the work was in Latin—"it is to the learned I address myself"— he could fairly claim that it was unlikely to disturb popular opinion. He never lacked courage, but he may have judged it impolitic, especially in the Restoration times, to publish what would have challenged orthodox opinion as held by both Anglicans and Puritans. After his death Daniel Skinner, to whom Milton left his manuscripts, made overtures to Elzevir for the treatise to be printed at Amsterdam, but the printer was nervous about its unorthodoxy and declined to print it, and Skinner, who by this time also became nervous, took no further steps. The treatise was lost sight of till it was discovered together with Milton's State Papers in 1823, and it was published two years later, edited with an English translation by Charles Sumner, a future Bishop of Winchester.

The difficulty of using the treatise freely for the interpretation of *Paradise Lost* lies in the uncertainty of the dates of its most important parts. From the fifteenth chapter of the first Book to the end of the work, the larger part of the manuscript is in the hand of Jeremie Picard, Milton's principal amanuensis during the years immediately preceding the Restoration; additions and corrections have been made in this Picard draft by many different hands, doubtless at Milton's dictation. The first fourteen chapters are in the hand of Daniel

Skinner, who, it has been suggested, copied these chapter afresh because the Picard draft of them was so much inte spersed with corrections that it would not serve as printer copy. We have no other version of these fourteen chapter except this final form, and it is open to doubt whether Milto had reached all the views expressed in them at the time whe he was composing at any rate the earlier Books of *Paradi Lost*. Those who hold that Milton had held such views su stantially for several years maintain that "the *De Doctrir* should be decisive in any question of interpreting" the epi and that it should be so used "freely and fully." Those wh judge from the alterations in the Picard draft that Milto was moving towards pronounced heterodoxy, and especial that the fifth chapter, "De Filio," in its final form, whic alone we have, represents a movement of Milton's theolog towards the left since he began *Paradise Lost*, think it unsa to interpret the poem by the treatise except with considerab reserve.

There is also a further consideration. It is one thing fe Milton to make an intellectual statement in a formal an scholastic treatise, and another to make such imaginativ use of Christian doctrine as will serve the poet when he "soaring in the high reason of his fancies, with his garlan and singing robes about him" (B., II, 477). If expressio in the poem are patient of an orthodox interpretation, it ma have been the poet's intention to leave his readers that libert of interpretation; a desire to commend his epic to the Englis public of his generation, as well as a sensible prudence, woul lead him to avoid challenging their religious convictions, he could do so without forfeiting his own intellectual integrit And, in fact, the great epic passed for orthodox with mo readers for a century and a half. It was sufficiently close the common Christian tradition to awake no suspicion their minds. The doctrines of the Incarnation and the Aton ment are stated without reserve, and the employment Scriptural terms in describing the divinity of the Son of G satisfied them of the author's substantial orthodoxy. The were, indeed, a few, both among those that resented an among those that welcomed it, who detected some expressio in the poem which approached the Arian view, and such suspicions were amply confirmed when the *De Doctrina* saw the light. The heterodoxy of the fifth chapter on the Son is incontrovertible, though it remains to be considered whether those heterodox opinions find expression in the poem.

It is essential to recognize that Milton professedly based his treatise on the Scriptures only. As completely as any Puritan of his time, he accepted the authority of the Bible as the only rule of faith, and he claimed the Protestant's right to interpret it for himself without any deference to tradition or any church. The truths of faith for him were

Left onely in those written Records pure,
Though not but by the Spirit understood.
(P.L., XII, 513.)

He was quite prepared to trust his own reason, after exercising all possible diligence, for the interpretation of the Bible, and he defends from the charge of heresy any who misunderstand the Scripture "after all sincere endeavours to understand it."

It is a human frailty to err, and no man is infallible here on earth. But so long as all these profess to set the Word of God only before them as the rule of faith and obedience; and use all diligence and sincerity of heart, by reading, by learning, by study, by prayer for illumination of the Holy Spirit, to understand the rule and obey it, they have done what man can do: God will assuredly pardon them, as he did the friends of Job. (B., II, 511.)

There is, however, one important qualification of Milton's professed dependence on the Bible only. He maintains that "we possess, as it were, a twofold Scripture, one external, which is the written word, and the other internal, which is the Holy Spirit, written in the hearts of believers," and "that which is internal, and the peculiar possession of each believer, is far superior to all, namely the Spirit itself" (B., IV, 447). Like other Puritans, his regard for the Old Testament was as reverential as for the New, except only that he came latterly to the view that the entire Mosaic law, and not the ceremonial only, was abrogated for Christians. Yet he put up a defence of polygamy because it had warrant in the Old Testament. In *Paradise Lost* the Almighty is more like Jehovah than the Heavenly Father of the Gospels.

The first and most essential article of the Nicene Creed— "I believe in one God the Father Almighty, maker of heaven and earth"—was held by Milton throughout life with unswerving loyalty. For him, as he states in the *De Doctrina* (B., IV, 87), "there is in reality but one true and supreme God," and "Christ agrees with the whole people of God, that the Father is that one and the only God." In the final position to which he comes in the treatise he allows a subordinate and derivative divinity to the Son, as his fidelity to the words of Scripture obliges him. The Holy Spirit is for him an influence rather than a Person. Orthodox theologians have always allowed some degree of subordination of the Son to the Father; the Son is declared in the creed to be "equal to the Father, as touching his Godhead, and inferior to the Father, as touching his manhood (*minor Patre secundum humanitatem*)." But Milton goes much farther in order to establish the subordination. Commenting on St. Paul's words concerning the Son that "all things were created through him," Milton maintains that "it must be understood of a secondary and delegated power"; the Father is the primary cause of Creation, the Son is "the secondary and instrumental cause" (B., IV, 91).

So far he could claim some orthodox support, but he goes farther. He argues that the Son, as Mediator, is necessarily inferior to the Father, whom He seeks to reconcile to men. He deliberately breaks with "received opinion" in denying the eternal generation of the Son, "begotten of his Father before all worlds." He allows that the Son was begotten by the decree of the Father before the angels or other created beings existed, but "within the limits of time" (84). He holds that New Testament passages "prove the existence of the Son before the world was made, but they conclude nothing respecting his generation from all eternity" (81). "God imparted to the Son as much as he pleased of the divine nature, nay, of the divine substance itself," but the Son is not "essentially one with the Father." "For when the Son is said to be *the first born of every creature,* and *the beginning of the creation of God,* nothing can be more evident than that God of his own will created, or generated, or produced the Son before all things, endued with the divine nature, as in the fulness of time he miraculously begat him in his human nature of the Virgin Mary" (85). The Son, he says, is not co-eval or co-essential with the Father, and he breaks with the credal terms that "the Godhead of the Father, of the Son, and of the Holy Ghost, is all one; the glory equal, the majesty co-eternal," and that the Son is "not made, nor created, but begotten."

In the treatise, addressed to scholars, he can draw out the full implications of his theology, but, if he had reached this position by the time he was writing *Paradise Lost,* he may not have thought it necessary or prudent to obtrude his personal heresies upon readers who were likely to be orthodox. It is well, therefore, to consider how the poem may have struck readers who had no knowledge of the treatise.

The third Book of *Paradise Lost,* in which the Son is first introduced, is little likely to have awoken suspicion. Seated beside "the Almighty Father," He shares with Him "high collateral glorie":

> on his right
> The radiant image of his Glory sat,
> His onely Son.
>
> (P.L., III, 62.)
>
> Beyond compare the Son of God was seen
> Most glorious, in him all his Father shon
> Substantially express'd, and in his face
> Divine compassion visibly appeerd,
> Love without end, and without measure Grace.
>
> (138.)

He is "the Son of God, In whom the fulness dwells of love divine," and "The great Creatour" addresses Him:

> O Son, in whom my Soul hath chief delight,
> Son of my bosom, Son who art alone
> My word, my wisdom, and effectual might,

All hast thou spok'n as my thoughts are, all
As my Eternal purpose hath decreed.

(168.)

And when the Son offers to become Man, "Made flesh,
when time shall be, of Virgin seed, By wondrous birth," He
is declared by the Father not to forfeit thereby His divinity:

Nor shalt thou by descending to assume
Mans Nature, less'n or degrade thine owne.
Because thou hast, though Thron'd in highest bliss
Equal to God, and equally enjoying
God-like fruition, quitted all to save
A World from utter loss, and hast been found
By Merit more than Birthright Son of God.

(303.)

After fulfilling His earthly mission, He shall at the end cite
the "dead of All past Ages to the general Doom" and "judge
Bad men and Angels," before laying down His office:

Then thou thy regal Scepter shalt lay by,
For regal Scepter then no more shall need,
God shall be All in All. But all ye Gods,
Adore him, who to compass all this dies,
Adore the Son, and honour him as mee.

(339.)

Accordingly, the command is fulfilled by the angels:

lowly reverent
Towards either Throne they bow, & to the ground
With solemn adoration down they cast
Thir Crowns inwove with Amarant and Gold.

(349.)

And if this ultimate surrender of regality denotes the subordination of the Son, Milton has the express warrant of St.
Paul's words: "And when all things shall be subdued unto
him, then shall the Son also himself be subject unto him that
put all things under him, that God may be all in all" (1 Cor.

xv. 28). Milton is entitled to put in the Son's mouth His willingness to fulfil the Father's will:

> Scepter and Power, thy giving, I assume,
> And gladlier shall resign, when in the end
> Thou shalt be All in All, and I in thee
> For ever, and in mee all whom thou lov'st.
>
> (VI, 730.)

The difficulties involved in dramatizing the Persons of the Trinity, and in assigning to them in the poem different actions and words, make any representation of the Unity in Trinity impossible, even if Milton was concerned to do so. When he introduces the word God, without further definition, he always intends the Father Almighty. And whatever high Scriptural language he uses about the Son, there is necessarily a visible distinction from the Supreme God. It has also the unfortunate effect of making the Son appeal more to the reader than the Father. There is a "strife of Mercy and Justice" in the face of the Father, and though He states that, in weighing their respective claims, "Mercy first and last shall brightest shine," His anger and threats, His insistence upon "rigid satisfaction" for "man's offence," and the hard legalistic tone of His speeches fastening blame upon fallen men and angels, make a more vivid impression than His mercy.

By contrast, the Son's willingness to endure the divine wrath in order to procure man's redemption calls out the angelic praise:

> O unexampl'd love,
> Love no where to be found less than Divine!
>
> (III, 410.)

And at this point the poet appears to speak in his own name, acclaiming the act of Redemption:

> Hail Son of God, Saviour of Men, thy Name
> Shall be the copious matter of my Song
> Henceforth, and never shall my Harp thy praise
> Forget, nor from thy Fathers praise disjoine.
>
> (III, 412.)

With this outburst may be compared the exclamation of
Adam on hearing from Michael the story of Redemption

> O goodness infinite, goodness immense!
> That all this good of evil shall produce,
> And evil turn to good; more wonderful
> Than that by which creation first brought forth
> Light out of darkness! full of doubt I stand,
> Whether I should repent me now of sin
> By mee done and occasiond, or rejoyce
> Much more, that much more good thereof shall spring,
> To God more glory, more good will to Men
> From God, and over wrauth grace shall abound.
>
> (XII, 469.)

The thought of Adam's sin occasioning the Incarnation and
the glorious work of Redemption is similar to that which is
so finely expressed, and with an even greater joyousness, in
the *O felix culpa* appointed in the missal to be sung on Easter
Even: "O surely necessary sin of Adam, which is blotted out
by the death of Christ! O happy fault, which has deserved
to have such and so mighty a Redeemer!" This emphasis
on Redemption is confirmed in the final words of the angelic
hymn after the Temptation in *Paradise Regained*:

> Hail Son of the most High, heir of both worlds,
> Queller of Satan, on thy glorious work
> Now enter, and begin to save mankind.
>
> (P.R., IV, 633.)

The pious reader of Milton's poems would be likely to be
satisfied by his treatment of this central theme of the Christian
faith. It is unlikely that, without knowledge of the *De Doctrina*
he would suspect any Arian tendency in the words of the
angelic praise of the Son which follows the praise of the
Father in Book III of *Paradise Lost*:

> Thee next they sang of all Creation first,
> Begotten Son, Divine Similitude,
> In whose conspicuous count'nance, without cloud
> Made visible, th' Almighty Father shines,
> Whom else no Creature can behold; on thee

Impresst the effulgence of his Glorie abides,
Transfus'd on thee his ample Spirit rests.
Hee Heav'n of Heavens and all the Powers therein
By thee created.

(III, 383.)

The first line would bring to the reader's mind St. Paul's
description of Christ as "the image of the invisible God, the
first-born of all creation" (Col. i. 15). This text has, indeed,
proved a difficult phrase in the history of Christian doctrine,
and the Arians of the fourth century took it to mean that
Christ was the first of all created beings, Himself a creature,
though the creed calls Him "not made, nor created." The
word "first-born" was probably used by St. Paul in the Old
Testament sense of the heir by virtue of primogeniture; it is
a word of constant use in the Old Testament, and in some
Rabbinic writings it is even used of the Almighty. The phrase
in *Paradise Lost* would pass muster with most of Milton's
readers because of its Pauline origin and associations, but we
know from the treatise that his personal view came to be
approximately Arian.

In Book V, where the Son is next introduced, the Father
appears to associate the Son with Himself on equal terms:

Son, thou in whom my glory I behold
In full resplendence, Heir of all my might,
Neerly it now concernes us to be sure
Of our Omnipotence, and with what Arms
We mean to hold what anciently we claim
Of Deitie or Empire, such a foe
Is rising, who intends to erect his Throne
Equal to ours.

(V, 716.)

These lines occur soon after the Father has declared to the
assembled angels His decree announcing His Son as Vice-
gerent. The announcement must be quoted in part, because it
has occasioned much discussion in recent books about Milton:

Hear all ye Angels, Progenie of Light,
Thrones, Dominations, Princedoms, Vertues, Powers,

Hear my Decree, which unrevok't shall stand.
This day I have begot whom I declare
My onely Son, and on this holy Hill
Him have anointed, whom ye now behold
At my right hand; your Head I him appoint;
And by my Self have sworn to him shall bow
All knees in Heav'n, and shall confess him Lord.

(V, 600.)

The crucial words, "This day I have begot," clearly relate to the citation from the second Psalm in the Epistle to the Hebrews (i. 5): "For unto which of the Angels said he at any time, Thou art my Son, this day have I begotten thee?" The Psalmist refers to a king's coronation, but the writer of the epistle applies it to the exaltation of the Son of God. Milton also must here be referring to the exaltation, not to the beginning of the Son in time, as in the same Book Abdiel reminds Satan that he and his fellow-angels owe their creation to the "begotten Son,"

by whom
As by his Word the mighty Father made
All things, ev'n thee, and all the Spirits of Heav'n
By him created in thir bright degrees.

(V, 832.)

Milton must be consistent with himself, at any rate within a few pages of the same Book. That he refers to the exaltation is also evident from the treatise, where he states that in Scripture the word *begotten* is used "in a double sense, the one literal, with reference to the production of the Son, the other metaphorical, with reference to his exaltation." And in citing the text from the Epistle to the Hebrews and similar texts, he says expressly that they "relate only to his metaphorical generation, that is, to his resuscitation from the dead, or to his unction to the mediatorial office, according to St. Paul's own interpretation of the second Psalm" (B., IV, 81). For the dramatic effectiveness of the poem he allows himself the poet's licence to place the exaltation, not at the Ascension, as the New Testament writers appear to place it, but before the fall of the angels so as to give Satan and his fellows, "the third part of Heavens host," and excuse for their resentment and rebellion. Satan himself

> yet fraught
> With envie against the Son of God, that day
> Honourd by his great Father, and proclaimd
> *Messiah* King anointed, could not beare
> Through pride that sight, and thought himself impaird.
>
> (V, 658).

In Book VII Raphael tells Adam at full length the story of the creation of the earth for man's habitation, and in that work the Son has the leading part. He is commissioned by the Almighty in these words:

> And thou my Word, begotten Son, by thee
> This I perform, speak thou, and be it don:
> My overshadowing Spirit and might with thee
> I send along, ride forth, and bid the Deep
> Within appointed bounds be Heav'n and Earth.
>
> (VII, 163.)

Already the rebel angels, so Abdiel states, had asserted that they "can allow Omnipotence to none," but the Father addresses the Son as "Second Omnipotence" (VI, 684). When the Son sets forth "on his great Expedition," "girt with Omnipotence," and "in Paternal Glorie rode Farr into Chaos and the World unborn," it is a little confusing to the reader to find that the Almighty, who has previously been described as remaining in heaven (VII, 163-6, 170), is also present with the Son. When we read "Let ther be Light, said God" (243), and similar quotations from *Genesis* on each of the succeeding days, we might naturally suppose it to be the *Fiat* of "God Supream." But we are in reasonable doubt because the Father's commission to the Son included the words, "speak thou, and be it don." On the sixth day of creation

> the Omnipotent
> Eternal Father (For where is not hee
> Present) thus to his Son audibly spake
> Let us make now Man in our image.
>
> (516.)

When the work of the sixth day is finished, "the great Creator" returned separately to heaven, "thence to behold this new created World." On the evening of the seventh day

The Filial Power arriv'd, and sate him down
With his great Father, for he also went
Invisible, yet staid (such priviledge
Hath Omnipresence) and the work ordain'd.

(587.)

The Father, then, is simultaneously in heaven and with His agent on earth. He plans "his great Idea" and commits its execution to the Son. This view of the Father as Creator and of the Son as His agent in creation has Scriptural warrant. St. Paul says of the Son that "all things were created through him" (Col. i. 15; the Vulgate has *omnia per ipsum*, not *ab ipso*, where the Authorized Version "by him" is misleading). In the *De Doctrina* creation "is always said to have taken place *per eum*, through him, not by him, but by the Father" (B., IV, 137).[1]

The passage in the later Books of *Paradise Lost* which most clearly reveals Milton's drift from orthodoxy occurs in Book VIII, where the Almighty, answering Adam's plea before the creation of Eve for some being to relieve his solitariness, puts to him His own case:

What thinkst thou then of mee, and this my State,
Seem I to thee sufficiently possest
Of happiness, or not? who am alone
From all Eternitie, for none I know
Second to mee or like, equal much less.
How have I then with whom to hold converse
Save with the Creatures which I made, and those
To me inferiour, infinite descents
Beneath what other Creatures are to thee?

(VIII, 403.)

The absence of any reference here to the Son is in striking

[1] The meaning of the very difficult passage, VII, 168-73, about God's "retraction"—"Though I uncircumscrib'd my self retire"—during the creation, cannot be satisfactorily discussed in this short book, but the reader is referred to Saurat, *Milton: Man and Thinker*, 1944, pp. 102-4, 231-47, and to criticism of Saurat's views in the books of Sewell and Kelley. Professor Saurat shows that Milton is borrowing from the Cabbalistic *Zohar*.

contrast to the words in Book III, where the Father addresses Him as "My sole complacence," "Thron'd in highest bliss Equal to God, and equally enjoying God-like fruition," words which echo St. Paul's description of "Christ Jesus, who, being in the form of God, thought it not robbery to be equal with God" (Phil. ii. 6). This text had evidently embarrassed Milton, and in the *De Doctrina* he hesitates as to whether it implies co-equality or not. (B., IV, 145.)

The Unity of God is an essential Christian doctrine and its harmony with the Trinity has always been difficult to state satisfactorily, and in the end Milton abandoned the attempt. In the mediæval folksong, "Green grow the rushes, O!", intended to teach the elements of Christian doctrine in a popular way, the number Three stands for the Trinity, and yet the song begins: "One is One, and all alone, and ever more shall be so." This might pass for orthodox, and countless readers of the passage in *Paradise Lost* have not detected that Milton had passed, or was passing, to a conception of the Son as a divine being subordinate to "God Supream," and of the Holy Spirit as an influence. On the whole, it is remarkable that he should have included so few hints of his departures from "received opinion" that his unorthodoxy was little suspected until the publication of the *De Doctrina*. His constant use of Scriptural language and the lofty attributes which he assigns to the Son and the emphasis on the central doctrine of the Redemption have reassured most of his readers who knew nothing of the treatise.[2]

[2] Other less important heresies are discoverable in *Paradise Lost*. For instance X, 782-93, and less certainly III, 245-6, point to Milton's being attracted to the Mortalist heresy, that the soul dies with the body, both awaiting the general resurrection. This is clearly stated in the *De Doctrina* (B., IV, 270), where he says: "as this is a subject which may be discussed without endangering our faith or devotion, whichever side of the controversy we espouse, I shall declare freely what seems to me the true doctrine, as collected from numberless passages of Scripture." He would regard it as a matter of opinion rather than a necessary article of faith.

Chapter 14

Milton's Doctrine of Man

MILTON'S DOCTRINE of man is almost as important as his doctrine of God, and the two are inextricably blended. In the highly theological temper of the seventeenth century even political and social writings commonly have a religious background, and this is especially true of Milton, whose religious interest is almost always evident on whatever matter he is writing.

It has already been noted that he based his "body of Divinity" on the systems of two Calvinist divines, one English and the other a Netherlander, and to the end the logical and austere theology of Calvin maintained some hold on his mind. In one important particular, however, he soon broke free from the full Calvinistic doctrine of predestination. With his fidelity to Scripture he must, indeed, pay some regard to St. Paul's use of the verb which the Authorized Version, following the Vulgate, translates *predestinate:* "For whom he did foreknow, he also did predestinate to be conformed to the image of his Son, that he might be the firstborn amongst many brethren. Moreover, whom he did predestinate, them he also called" (Rom. viii. 28-9). The theological term "Predestination" was used to describe God's foreordaining by an eternal decree or purpose some men through grace to salvation and everlasting life, and, though this was not included in the doctrine by all theologians, foreordaining others to perdition. Thus the Westminster Assembly in 1647 defined it in their Confession: "By the decree of God, for the manifestation of His glory, some men and angels are predestined unto everlasting life, and others foreordained to everlasting death." Archbishop Whitgift's Lambeth Articles of 1595, which Queen Elizabeth's good sense saved from being imposed on the Church of England, asserted: "God from eternity hath predestinated some to life, some He hath reprobated to death."

The idea of God's calling or election of some men was not unpalatable to Milton. He never questioned that he was himself among the Elect, chosen of God to a lofty destiny. Whether we approve the doctrine or not, we cannot fail to see that this side of the Calvinistic creed was a very powerful incentive in the life of the typical Puritan, of Cromwell no less than of Milton. To believe that he is destined and called to fulfil the purpose of God, and that he is assured of divine grace to uphold him in this life and of salvation hereafter, is enough to give a man courage and inflexible resolution; he can face opposition and obloquy and apparent failure with faith unshaken. That is the real strength of the Calvinistic faith, and it is illustrated in the lives and characters of the best Puritans, not least in Milton himself. When the Almighty in *Paradise Lost* declares His "Eternal purpose" for mankind, He utters words to which the poet could give full assent:

> Some I have chosen of peculiar grace
> Elect above the rest; so is my will.
>
> (III, 183.)

That the Elect might be few would not dismay Milton. In his political thinking, too, he came to distrust the people; his aristocratic temper had only so much of democratic feeling that he admonished the wise few to govern in the interest of the unfit many. Similarly, the Christ of *Paradise Regained* expresses His scorn for "the people" who are "a herd confus'd, a miscellaneous rabble" (P.R., III, 47-59).

But Milton was unable to assent to the doctrine of preordained perdition. In the *De Doctrina* he says roundly: "none can be reprobated, except they do not believe or continue in the faith, and even this rather as a consequence than a decree; there can therefore be no reprobation of individuals from all eternity" (B, IV, 64). He maintains, as will be now generally thought rightly, that there is no warrant from Scripture that "reprobation is an absolute decree"; even reprobation "is rescinded by repentance," so that it is contingent only. In agreement with the treatise, the Almighty is represented in the poem as continuing, after He has spoken of the Elect, with these words:

> The rest shall hear me call, and oft be warnd
> Thir sinful state, and to appease betimes

> Th' incensed Deitie while offerd grace
> Invites; for I will cleer thir senses dark,
> What may suffice, and soft'n stonie hearts
> To pray, repent, and bring obedience due.
> To prayer, repentance, and obedience due,
> Though but endevord with sincere intent,
> Mine eare shall not be slow, mine eye not shut.
>
> (III, 184.)

And in the treatise, in opposition to much Puritan teaching, Milton maintains that the ransom paid by Christ "is in itself sufficient for the redemption of all mankind, all are called to partake of its benefits" (B., IV, 321).

It was not only that unconditional and inescapable reprobation offended Milton's sense of justice and dangerously emphasized the arbitrary nature of the Omnipotent's dealings with mankind, but it was also incompatible with Milton's dearly prized conception of man's free will. With his rugged individualism and confidence in his own powers, he clung almost fiercely to his belief in free will. Again and again in *Paradise Lost* he stresses the freedom of choice which God has given to man and man's sole accountability for his acts. If choice is not real but determined, he urges, there is no virtue in obedience and no just cause of censure and punishment for disobedience.

Milton had used this argument long before in *Aeropagitica*, when he placed the man of tried virtue who had resisted temptation high above the merely innocent, whose sheltered lives had protected them from falling but had also debarred them from achieving any virtue deserving of praise. In *Paradise Lost* the Almighty holds man to blame for abusing his freedom of choice:

> I made him just and right,
> Sufficient to have stood, though free to fall.
> Such I created all th' Ethereal Powers
> And Spirits, both them who stood & them who faild;
> Freely they stood who stood, and fell who fell.
>
> (III, 98.)

Raphael bids Adam "be advis'd" of his freedom and of the moral value that alone attaches to freely chosen obedience:

God made thee perfet, not immutable;
And good he made thee, but to persevere
He left it in thy power, ordaind thy will
By nature free, not overrul'd by Fate
Inextricable, or strict necessity;
Our voluntarie service he requires,
Not our necessitated, such with him
Findes no acceptance, nor can find, for how
Can hearts, not free, be tri'd whether they serve
Willing or no, who will but what they must
By Destinie, and can no other choose?

(V, 524.)

The archangel says of his fellow-angels too: "freely we serve
Because wee freely love." And in his last counsel to Adam
he says:

I in thy persevering shall rejoyce,
And all the Blest: stand fast; to stand or fall
Free in thine own Arbitrement it lies.

(VIII, 639.)

Adam in turn passes on this counsel to Eve:

But God left free the Will, for what obeyes
Reason, is free, and Reason he made right
But bid her well beware, and still erect,
Least by some faire appeering good surpris'd
She dictate false, and missinforme the Will
To do what God expressly hath forbid.

(IX, 351.)

It is evident from this repeated emphasis how much importance Milton attached to the idea of free will, and it agrees closely with his own character and attitude to life. Conscious of his habit of making deliberate choice at every step in his political and literary career, and bravely prepared to abide by the consequences, whether he was supported or traduced by public opinion, this man of iron will took his line and believed that salvation lay in others doing the like. If his self-confidence was greater than that of other men, and if, like

Abdiel, he was ready to stand alone, it is significant that Raphael commends a proper self-esteem:

> Oft times nothing profits more
> Than self-esteem, grounded on just and right
> Well manag'd.

(VIII, 571.)

And Milton admits to having himself "a certain niceness of nature, an honest haughtiness, and self-esteem either of what I was, or what I might be" (B., III, 118).

Milton was fully conscious of the difficulty of harmonizing any even modified doctrine of predestination or of God's foreknowledge with man's freedom. It was a question endlessly debated in the seventeenth century, and he probably has the divines of the Westminster Assembly in mind when he describes a group of fallen angels "on a Hill retir'd" employing their leisure in profitless discussion

> Of Providence, Foreknowledge, Will, and Fate,
> Fixt Fate, free will, foreknowledge absolute,
> And found no end, in wandring mazes lost.

(II, 559.)

The difficulty does not deter him from assaying a solution of this insoluble problem in the lengthy argument of the Almighty when, in foretelling men's disobedience, He is concerned to establish that they were not predestined to sin and its penalties by any "absolute Decree":

> They therefore as to right belongd,
> So were created, nor can justly accuse
> Thir maker, or thir making, or thir Fate;
> As if Predestination over-rul'd
> Thir will, dispos'd by absolute Decree
> Or high foreknowledge; they themselves decreed
> Thir own revolt, not I: if I foreknew,
> Foreknowledge had no influence on their fault,
> Which had no less prov'd certain unforeknown.
> So without least impulse or shadow of Fate,
> Or aught by me immutablie foreseen,

They trespass, Authors to themselves in all
Both what they judge and what they choose; for so
I formed them free, and free they must remain,
Till they enthrall themselves: I else must change
Thir nature.

(III, 111.)

And when Adam fell, "the most High Eternal Father" declares that it was his own undoing, "no Decree of mine Concurring to necessitate his Fall" (X, 43).

Milton had also to find room in the poem and the treatise for the doctrine of Grace. He must at least pay formal deference to the Scriptural teaching of man's need of divine Grace to enable him to recover from his fall:

Man shall not quite be lost, but sav'd who will,
Yet not of will in him, but grace in me
Freely voutsaft; once more I will renew
His lapsed powers, though forfeit and enthrall'd
By sin to foul exorbitant desires.

(III, 173.)

And in the treatise Milton says: "the natural mind and will of man being partially renewed by a Divine impulse are led to seek the knowledge of God. . . . Inasmuch as this change is from God, those in whom it takes place are said to be enlightened, and to be endued with power to will what is good" (B., IV, 323). The word *partially* sounds a little grudging, as if Milton's self-sufficiency is strained to make this concession, but it is explained when he says that "all exhortation would be addressed in vain" to those "who were not endued with some portion of mental judgement and liberty of will" (326). The intent of "renovation" is to "infuse from above new and supernatural faculties into the minds of the renovated"; "if the will of the regenerate be not made free, then we are not renewed, but compelled to embrace salvation in an unregenerate state" (329). Even salvation is not welcome to John Milton if it impairs his freedom of will.

Milton connects his idea of freedom with the Gospel. Christian liberty, he says, is "the fundamental privilege of the

Gospel, the new birthright of every true believer" (B., II, 539). Since the coming of "Christ our deliverer," "liberty must be considered as belonging in an especial manner to the Gospel, and as consorting therewith" (B., IV, 398). These words in the treatise are exactly paralleled in *Paradise Lost* where Michael foresees the forcers of conscience in the history of the Church:

> What will they then
> But force the Spirit of Grace it self, and binde
> His consort Libertie; what, but unbuild
> His living Temples, built by Faith to stand,
> Thir own Faith not anothers: for on Earth
> Who against Faith and Conscience can be heard
> Infallible? yet many will presume:
> Whence heavie persecution shall arise
> On all who in the worship persevere
> Of Spirit and Truth.
>
> (P.L., XII, 524.)

Yet, supremely as Milton values freedom, he realizes that true freedom lies in obedience to the will of God, and that disobedience means servitude. The theme of the epic is "Mans First Disobedience" that wrought "all our woe." Disobedience brought thraldom, and there is no recovery save by redirection of the will. Milton, with his own resolute nature, is always tempted to think that man's recovery is within his own power. Man has but to give the reason control over the passions, as Adam and Samson failed to do, and as Christ the "greater Man" successfully did in the Temptation, and all will be well. "Reason," says the Almighty, "is choice" (P.L., III, 108), and Will is the power of putting reason into action. Milton tends to think that a right use of reason is sufficient and possible. There are, however, some indications of the bitter experiences of life having taught him that, for others if not for himself, human nature unaided cannot renew its will to good without spiritual assistance from outside, the initiative to reform or regeneration coming to him from God. Adam and Eve after the Fall are enabled to repent,

> for from the Mercie-seat above
> Prevenient Grace descending had remov'd
> The stonie from thir hearts, and made new flesh
> Regenerate grow instead.
>
> (XI, 2.)

Much as he generally objects to "scholastic notions," Milton has recourse to the technical term "Prevenient Grace," which denotes the divine Grace preceding repentance and conversion, and predisposing the heart before it is turning Godwards of its own motion. This Grace is not, as Calvinists were wont to say, irresistible; it cannot coerce but only persuade, so that there is still room for the human will to respond and cooperate. Milton's sturdy individualism makes him careful to safeguard his freedom even in receiving divine assistance.

The same very English individualism makes him suspicious of dependence upon any church with its ministers and their ministrations. The sacraments receive very perfunctory notice in the *De Doctrina,* and their use is left to the option of those who care to use them rather than that they should be regarded as normal means of grace. Ministers, whether Roman or Anglican or Presbyterian, come in for harsh criticism throughout the prose treatises and in Michael's prophecy of the Christian Church in the last Book of *Paradise Lost.* Milton is even uncertain whether ministers are wanted at all; he is sure that they need no university training or State support; and if they continue, they can be left to depend on their flocks for support, and the money from public sources spent on their maintenance would be better spent on the education of the laity. This is "the likeliest means to remove Hirelings out of the Church."

He is doubtful of the value of church buildings; "notwithstanding the gaudy superstition of some devoted still ignorantly to temples," he writes in the last year of the Protectorate, "a house or barn" would serve as well for those who are minded "to meet and edify one another" (B., III, 26). He scouts the notion of consecrated buildings, for holiness is not in place at all. When Adam laments that, on his expulsion from Paradise,

This most afflicts me, that departing hence,
As from his face I shall be hid, deprivd
His blessed count'nance; here I could frequent,
With worship, place by place where he voutsaf'd
Presence Divine, and to my Sons relate;

(XI, 315.)

he is answered by Michael:

Yet doubt not but in Vallie and in Plaine
God is as here, and will be found alike
Present, and of his presence many a signe
Still following thee, still compassing thee round
With goodness and paternal Love.

(XI, 349.)

Milton has all the Puritan intolerance of any ceremonial forms of worship. He is not only anti-clerical but anti-ecclesiastical. He could nourish his genuine religious faith by private meditation and by his assiduous study of the Bible, and needed for himself no other means of grace. His was a personal, not a corporate, religion; for a poet he was singularly little touched with any mystical feeling, and for a scholar he has less regard for Christian tradition than any who have studied and written much upon theology. Yet there is no mistaking the genuineness of his religion throughout life; at the close, in spite of all frustration and disillusion, he could have appropriated to himself the invincible faith that he attributes to his Samson: "My trust is in the living God."

It remains to estimate briefly the influence upon his character of his strongly held opinions about God and man. They were not of a kind to correct a certain hardness which belonged to him of nature. He was more at home in the Old Testament than in the New, and even in the older Scriptures he draws more from the historical books than, as we might have expected of a poet, from Isaiah and the Psalms. In the New Testament he finds the Pauline epistles more to his mind than the Gospels. The Son of God in *Paradise Lost* is, indeed, reverenced for the sacrificial love which moved Him to the work of Redemption, but He is also graphically portrayed at the head of His legions "with his Chariot and Thunder driving into the midst of his Enemies," like the Word of God in the Apocalypse, "clothed with a vesture dipt in blood," riding forth to "smite the nations" and to tread "the winepress of the fierceness and wrath of Almighty God."

The moral earnestness of Milton is always evident in everything that he wrote as well as in his life. He believed himself to be, and always acted and wrote as one who was, in fact, a servant of righteousness. This conviction gave him a courage that cannot but be heartily admired, and an assurance that, though his own efforts for the cause he advocated should be frustrated, the cause itself was certain of ultimate victory because it was God's cause. If this assurance made him unjust to his opponents, and apt to be censorious, this was a penalty that could hardly be escaped by a man of such passionate convictions. His belief in England was tempered by bitter experience, but it still stood, though he saw that the struggle for freedom would need to be renewed by other Englishmen after his day. In his own generation he played his part manfully, even heroically, and left an example to his countrymen.

The high conscientiousness of the man John Milton had its effects on him as poet also. No English poet prepared himself for his poetic achievements with more thoroughness, and none has exercised his craft with such unremitting care. He is the greatest craftsman of all the English poets; save for a few of the occasional verses, to which he attached little importance, he maintains throughout the great volume of his poetry the same high standard of noble diction, melodious verse and accomplished workmanship. Dr. Johnson's judgment that "the characteristick quality of his poem is sublimity" is corroborated by Addison's remark that "Milton's chief talent, and indeed his distinguishing excellence, lies in the sublimity of his thoughts." Frederick Denison Maurice said of *Paradise Lost* that it comes to us "as a voice which can make the deepest mind of a grand age of English History intelligible to us." For the interpretation of that age Milton is as necessary to us as Cromwell and Hampden, Strafford and Falkland.

Besides the monumental poems of Milton's full powers, there is the delicate perfection of such shorter poems as the ode "At a Solemn Musick," *Lycidas,* and the sonnets. They are endeared to many readers whose patience fails to sustain them through the long poems or whose sympathy is alienated by Milton's Puritan theology. Some of the sonnets are among the best ever written in the English language, and they inspired another great poet to use that form with better effect than any poet since Milton, and often for the same political purpose as Milton had used it. Dorothy Wordsworth often read *Paradise Lost* aloud to her brother in the evenings, and one day in May 1802 she records in her *Journal* that she read Milton's sonnets, and within a few days William, who had never used that form before except for a boyish attempt "wrote two sonnets on Buonaparte." In the next few months Wordsworth was writing many of the magnificent sonnets which he afterwards collected in "Poems dedicated to National Independence and Liberty." In September of that year he wrote the sonnet beginning "Milton! thou shouldst be living at this hour: England hath need of thee," with its splendid tribute to the elder poet:

> Thy soul was like a Star, and dwelt apart;
> Thou hadst a voice whose sound was like the sea;
> Pure as the naked heavens, majestic, free.

A little later, in a sonnet on British freedom, he exclaims in words which would have fortified the faith and warmed the heart of the proud Milton himself:

> We must be free or die, who speak the tongue
> That Shakespeare spake: the faith and morals hold
> Which Milton held.

And it was Milton's use of the sonnet for lofty political ideals, as in the one "On the late Massacher in Piemont," which moved Wordsworth to the defence of "the Sonnet's scanty plot of ground":

> when a damp
> Fell round the path of Milton, in his hand
> The Thing became a trumpet; whence he blew
> Soul-animating strains—alas, too few!

Epilogue

JOHN MILTON has earned his place in the history of the English people. Ideas, nobly expressed, have a longer and more potent life than the actions of men: "a good book is the precious life-blood of a master-spirit, embalmed and treasured up on purpose to a life beyond life." Napoleon, the supreme example of the man of action, confessed as much to a friend when his active life was ended:

> Fontanes, do you know what I wonder at most in the world? The impotence of force to organise anything. There are only two powers in the world, the sabre and the mind. In the end the sabre is always beaten by the mind.

And the ideas which Milton expressed were, most of them, especially representative of the English mind. Above all, there is his lifelong concern for freedom in every department of life—personal and national, intellectual and religious. Again, his habit of viewing every question, political and religious, in its moral aspect is characteristically English, as foreigners have always observed, not always without suspicion.

Milton is also very English in his sturdy individualism. He claimed and exercised the right to think for himself, to form his own political judgments, and to interpret the Scriptures in his own way with singularly little regard for tradition or authority. He was not free from the defects of such unqualified individualism. While he could generally find those who were able *idem sentire de republica,* to agree with his political sentiments, and associated himself with their activities, he could never for long attach himself to any religious communion, in spite of religion being his dominant concern. At all costs he must preserve his intellectual integrity, and he uttered his convictions on matters of Church and State with small concern for his personal safety or reputation.

As Oliver Cromwell is the greatest representative of Puritanism in the field of action, Milton is in the sphere of thought. Most fair-minded Englishmen will allow that the Puritan strain in English history has done more to ennoble and strengthen our national life than to debase and weaken it. Milton's whole-hearted adoption of the Puritan cause necessarily qualifies the esteem of Englishmen who do not share his political and religious convictions, but we should have thought the worse of him if, when grave national issues were to be decided, he had proudly stood aloof and cried with Mercutio, "A plague o' both your Houses." Yet inevitably his vehement partisanship makes his appeal less universal than that of Shakespeare, who had a larger share of the touch of nature which makes the whole world kin.

When he had already won European fame by his Latin *Defences of the English People* and might have increased that fame by continuing to use that language, he rightly decided to do all possible honour to the mother tongue by employing it for his highest task. No poet ever wrought with such unceasing care to give the utmost dignity to the English language. "What other author," asks Dr. Johnson, "ever soared so high, or sustained his flight so long?" There are, indeed, some critics in our time who complain that there is monotony in this sustained elevation of style and that the Miltonic diction is too far removed from the language of common speech. It is, however, his own individual style, which he believed to be best suited to his majestic theme. The common judgment of the last two centuries is not likely to be reversed by a passing mood of criticism; *securus iudicat orbis terrarum.*

Most lovers of our English literature will agree with the poet Gray in placing Milton next after Shakespeare:

> Nor second He, that rode sublime
> Upon the seraph-wings of Ecstasy,
> The secrets of th' Abyss to spy.
> He passed the flaming bounds of Place and Time;
> The living Throne, the sapphire-blaze,
> Where Angels tremble, while they gaze,
> He saw; but, blasted with excess of light,
> Closed his eyes in endless night.

Such sublimity as Milton achieved in *Paradise Lost* could have proceeded only from a mind and character that had something of true nobility. The courage and tenacity of purpose with which he undertook his great work in spite of blindness and adversity will always command the admiration of Englishmen. "He was born," says Johnson, "for whatever is arduous"; there is an heroic quality in the temper and proud independence of the blind poet. He could turn even his affliction to advantage, as he himself claimed in the fine autobiographical passage at the beginning of the third Book of the epic, and as others have gladly recognized. Wordsworth had not only Homer and Tiresias in mind, but also his own countryman when he wrote of man's "imperishable spirit":

> Unto the men who see not as we see
> Futurity was thought, in ancient times,
> To be laid open, and they prophesied.
> And know we not that from the blind have flowed
> The highest, holiest, raptures of the lyre;
> And wisdom married to immortal verse?

Further Reading

The most useful edition of the Poetical Works is in the Oxford Standard Authors series, edited from the original texts by H. C. Beeching (revised, 1938); translations are given of the Latin, Greek, and Italian poems, and there is a Reader's Guide to unfamiliar words and proper names. The Cambridge University Press has *Paradise Lost* with full notes and glossary by A. W. Verity, who has also annotated the earlier poems and *Samson Agonistes*. L. C. Martin has edited *Paradise Regained* (Oxford, 1925), and J. S. Smart has edited the *Sonnets* (Maclehose, Glasgow, 1921).

The most complete collection of Milton's *Works,* in verse and prose, is the Columbia University edition in eighteen volumes (1931-8), but its cost, £24, places it out of the reach of most students except in libraries; a very comprehensive Index in two volumes followed in 1940. A convenient edition of the *Prose Works* is in Bohn's Standard Library, five volumes (1848-53), which may often be picked up second-hand. Selections of the more important prose works are in the World's Classics (No. 293) and in Everyman's Library (No. 795). P. B. and E. M. W. Tillyard have edited and translated from the Latin *Milton's Private Correspondence and Academic Exercises* (1932).

The chief authentic sources of biography are collected in *The Early Lives of Milton,* edited by Helen Darbishire (Constable, 1932). D. Masson's *Life of John Milton,* seven volumes (1859-94), is a quarry of information, but its bias must be allowed for. Samuel Johnson's "Milton" in *The Lives of the English Poets* should not be neglected, in spite of his prejudices and limitations. Among the many modern lives may be mentioned those by Mark Pattison (English Men of Letters series, 1879), Raleigh (1900), John Bailey (1915); also there are valuable studies in E. Dowden, *Puritan and Anglican* (1900), L. Abercrombie, *The Epic* (1914), Robert Bridges, *Milton's Prosody* (revised edition, 1921), and J. H. Hanford, *A Milton Handbook* (1928).

Among recent studies are Tillyard, *Milton* (1930), T. S. Eliot, *Selected Essays* (1932), F. R. Leavis, *Revaluations* (1936), Sir H. J. C. Grierson, *Milton and Wordsworth* (1937), L. Pearsall Smith, *Milton and his Modern Critics* (1940), C. S. Lewis, *A Preface to Paradise Lost* (1942), D. Saurat, *Milton: Man and Thinker* (revised 1944), C. M. Bowra, *From Virgil to Milton* (1945) and Douglas Bush, *Paradise Lost in our Time* (1946).

Sumner's translation (1825) of *De Doctrina Christiana* is reprinted in Volumes IV and V of Bohn's edition of the *Prose Works*. A. Sewell, *A Study in Milton's Christian Doctrine* (1939) and M. Kelley, *The Great Argument* (Princeton, 1941) discuss from different points of view the bearings of *De Doctrina Christiana* on the interpretation of *Paradise Lost*. Z. S. Fink, *The Classical Republicans* (Northwestern University, Evanston, U.S.A., 1945) discusses Milton's political thinking.

Index

Index